# WORSHIP

# AS YOU LIKE IT?

**SOTIRIOS CHRISTOU**

Other books by Sotirios Christou

The Priest & The People Of God – 2003

Evangelism & Collaborative Ministry – 2004

Anglican & Beyond Repair? – 2005

Paul & The Unsearchable Riches Of Christ – 2006

Published by Phoenix Books – Cambridge
Front cover – stained glass  window in
memory of Alan E. Lewis. McMillan
Building – Austin Presbyterian
Theological Seminary

We pray to You, O God, who are the supreme Truth,
    and all truth is from You.
We beseech You, O God, who are the highest Wisdom,
    and all the wise depend on You for their wisdom.
You are the supreme Joy, and all who are joyful owe it to you.
You are the greatest Good, and all goodness comes from You.
You are the Light of minds, and all receive their understanding
    from You.

We love You – indeed, we love You above all things.
We seek You, follow You and are prepared to serve You.

*Alfred The Great, King Of England – 849-899*


Almighty God
To whom all hearts are open,
All desires known
And from whom no secrets are hidden:
Cleanse the thoughts of our hearts
By the inspiration of your Holy Spirit,
That we may perfectly love you
And worthily magnify your holy name:
Through Jesus Christ our Lord. Amen.

*Cranmer's Collect For Purity*

# CONTENTS

# CHAPTER THREE

## THE PSALMS AND WORSHIP

# CHAPTER FOUR

## CHRIST AND WORSHIP

# CHAPTER FIVE

## WORSHIP AT THE THRONE OF GOD

# CHAPTER SIX

## CONTEMPORARY & CHARISMATIC WORSHIP

# CHAPTER SEVEN

## THE WISE SCRIBE

# INTRODUCTION

When I had my call for ministry tested in the Church of England in 1981, I went with a simple trust that this was what the Lord was calling me to. During a Selection Conference over two days I was interviewed by three selectors, who had the authority to recommend to my bishop whether or not I should train for ministry in the Church of England. One of the most constructive and helpful points the selectors raised, was that they wanted me to show an 'intellectual curiosity.' Intellectual curiosity cultivates an inquiring mind and invites us to ask searching questions about the Christian faith – that can deepen our faith.

The inspiration behind this book reflects an inquiring mind that seeks to identify biblical principles of worship, and also looks to see how these might be relevant to contemporary and charismatic worship. Churches who espouse these styles of worship are likely to have members who attend 'New Wine,' 'Soul Survivor' and 'Spring Harvest.' My hope is that my biblical studies along with my research will help us to be better informed about worship. And I trust this will also enable us to understand the dynamics, the history and the theology of contemporary and charismatic worship.

Jonathan Gledhill the Bishop of Litchfield sums up the wonder of Christian worship when he says:

> Worship is the response of the creature to the Creator: to worship is the desire to give true worth to what is beyond our powers of appreciation. To worship is to be aware of the heavens declaring the glory of God: to worship is to be aware of the transcendence of God: the infinite distance between the Maker and the made: and at the same time His immanence: to be part of a creation that longs to respond more properly to God at work within it.[1]

This captures the wonder and transcendence of God that inspires us to worship Him. We are probably aware that the origin in English of the word worship is 'worthship' which expresses value – the worth placed on someone or something. Graham Kendrick refers to the word '*proskuneo*' as the most commonly used word to describe worship in the New Testament, which means 'to come forward to kiss' (the hand) and it denotes both the external act of prostrating oneself in worship and the corresponding inward act of reverence and humility.'[2]

The weakness of the derivation 'worthship' is that it depends on people making a subjective assessment of God's worth. David Peterson, the Principal of Oakhill Theological College, echoes this when he says: 'Worship means by derivation to 'attribute worth' which suggests that to worship God is to ascribe him supreme worth...But worship interpreted and understood in this way may not have anything to do at all with the particularity of biblical revelation.'[3]

Peterson's understanding of what constitutes worship leads him to say: 'While worship is often broadly defined as our response to God – there is an important theological context to be considered when worship is presented in such terms...At one level we must discover from God's own self-revelation in Scripture what pleases him. We cannot determine for ourselves what is honouring to him. In particular we need to take seriously the extraordinary biblical perspective that acceptable worship is something made possible for us by God.'[4] We come to worship God according to the biblical principles he has given us and these should reflect the essence of our different styles of worship. Peterson echoes this when he says: 'The worship of the true and living God is essentially an engagement with him on the terms that he proposes and in the way he alone makes possible.'[5]

Archbishop William Temple has a challenging definition of Christian worship, that shows how every aspect of our being is involved in worship.

> Worship is the submission of all our nature to God. It is the quickening of the conscience by His holiness: the nourishment of the mind with His truth: the purifying of the imagination by His beauty: the opening of the heart to His love: the surrender of the will to His purpose – and all this gathered up in adoration, the most selfless emotion of which our nature is capable.[6]

But a definition of Christian worship also has to include Christ or it would be incomplete. Christopher Cocksworth, the Principal of Ridley Hall in Cambridge, in 'Holy, Holy, Holy – Worshipping The Trinitarian God' – shares how during his ordination training each member in his tutorial group was asked to give a definition of worship in one sentence. At the time he was working for a research degree in the area of Christian worship and gave what he thought was a suitably sophisticated answer. 'It was something on the lines of offering our whole lives to God in grateful self-giving. But, along with others in the group, I was much more moved by the answer of a young Church of Scotland ordinand on an exchange visit to the college. 'For me' he said 'worship is joining with Jesus as he praises his Father.' He made the reality of Christian existence and the nature of Christian prayer and worship startlingly clear and simple. To be a Christian is to be in Christ through his Spirit. To relate to God in prayer and worship is to do so *in, through* and even *with* Christ.'[7]

John White draws our attention to Professor Hoon who emphasises the Christological center of Christian worship – which 'by definition is Christological – and the analysis of the meaning of worship likewise must be fundamentally Christological.'

Such worship is profoundly incarnational in being governed by the whole event of Jesus Christ. Christian worship is bound directly to the events of salvation history while bridging them and bringing them into our present. The core of worship is God acting to give His life to man and to bring man to partake of that life. Hence all we do as individuals or as the church is affected by worship.

Christian worship is God's revelation of himself in Jesus Christ and man's response – or a twofold action – that of God towards the human soul in Jesus Christ and in man's responsive action through Jesus Christ. Through His Word God discloses and communicates His very being to man.[8]

White perceives that the key words in Hoon's understanding of Christian worship seem to be 'revelation' and 'response.' At the center of both is Jesus Christ – who reveals God to us and through whom we make our response.[9]

At the same time a definition of Christian worship that did not include a reference to the Holy Spirit would be lacking. C. Cocksworth says: 'The Spirit is the one who enables us to worship because the Spirit brings us into fellowship with Christ and therefore with each other and with his Father. As we worship we enter into the movement of Christ's self-giving to the Father through the Spirit...as our worship is communion with the Son and the Father in the Spirit and because we worship the God whose being is the communion of Father, Son and Holy Spirit, worship cannot be something we do independently of others. Father, Son and Spirit are not isolated individuals doing their own thing.'[10] 'Christian worship is participation in the eventful life of God through the presence and activity of the Holy Spirit in the life of the believer and in the midst of the fellowship of the Church.'[11]

'The confidence that God has given the Spirit to the Church should not lead us to complacent assurance that authentic worship will automatically happen simply by virtue of the fact we are the Church. It should compel us to enter more deeply into the gift God has given so that our worship can be truly inspired, by virtue of the fact that the Spirit is breaking us out of our preoccupation with ourselves and taking us into the love which Christ has for God.'[12]

In 'Worship At The Next Level' – there is an emphasis on Trinitarian worship – James Torrance describes this as: 'our participation through the Spirit in the Son's Communion with the Father in his vicarious life of worship and intercession.'[13] 'Because Christian worship by definition is our participation in the life of the triune God, worship simultaneously expresses our theology and shapes it. Therefore our worship must be 'intelligent' – using our minds (as well as our hearts, voices and bodies). Worship leaders are some of the church's primary theological educators and they need to work through the theological and cultural truths involved in worship. Torrance presses the point:

> If our worship is to be intelligent, offered joyfully in the freedom of the Spirit, we must look at the realities which inspire us and demand from us an intelligent, meaningful response. As theological educators it is therefore essential that those leading worship be theologically, culturally and aesthetically educated.'[14]

One of the challenges of contemporary worship is not to become complacent but to have inquiring minds that desire to learn more about the dynamics, the theology and the Trinitarian essence of worship. For most people whatever their tradition of worship is, it will be relatively predictable. I hope that my biblical studies and research will encourage an intellectual and spiritual curiosity to learn more about the biblical principles of worship that can inform and shape our different styles. We can invoke the Holy Spirit to help us in our desire to deepen our corporate worship. In response the Spirit will lead us on a journey that will enrich it.

'Living In Praise – Worshipping & Knowing God' by D. F. Ford, Regius Professor of Divinity at the University of Cambridge and D. W. Hardy, former Director of The Center of Theological Inquiry in Princeton, New Jersey – is an interesting and thought provoking book. In this the authors focus on the significance of the praise of God as central to the whole of life. In chapter two they begin with the concept of praise being what we express when we find something of quality and declare our appreciation – and that doing so adds something to the situation. They point out that this is true when we praise a person. 'To recognise worth and to respond to it with praise is to create a new relationship. This new mutual delight is itself something of worth, an enhancement of what was already valued.'[15]

The authors share their belief that this can continue in an infinite spiral of free response and expression and like lovers the declaration of appreciation is not an optional extra in the relationship, but is intrinsic to its quality and vitality. When respect and mutual delight that are at the heart of praise continually overflow, this brings freedom in a relationship and becomes the way of self-transcendence in thought, word and act. This desire to delight in another person can bring an awakening of new responses that yearn to express in greater abundance their love and appreciation of the uniqueness of that person. In this context the logic of praise is that it results in an overflow of freedom and generosity.[16] What is striking about their train of thought is that it speaks to us about the praise and worship of God – being the overflow of a heart that has been captured and won over by the love of God and Christ. To deepen our corporate praise and worship a good place to start is to invoke the Holy Spirit to fill our hearts in a new way with the love of God and Christ: and to pray that our souls may be captivated by them – so that this may draw forth from God's people an overflow of praise and worship.

The authors also allude to Dante's pilgrimage of praise and worship that began in Florence when he met Beatrice when they were both children. Dante says: 'the young are subject to a 'stupor' or astonishment of the mind which falls on them at the awareness of great and wonderful things. Such a stupor produces two results – a sense of reverence and a desire to know more. A noble awe and a noble curiosity come to life.' This is what happened to him at the sight of the Florentine girl, and all this work consists one way or another in the increase of that worship and that knowledge.[17]

Ford and Hardy point out that Dante was in love with Beatrice and as a young man wrote poetry about his love for her. When she died the vision he had seen through her inspired the Divine Comedy. His experience of falling in love was taken up into the vision of being transformed and led him to write the last canto of the Paradiso. 'To arrive at this he went through an experience of recognising his own sin and being humbled that radically changed the tone of his later poetry. His praise is the other side of a humility in which he sees himself realistically in relation to Beatrice and to God. What is striking is that Dante's progress through heaven continually astonishes in its ability to describe even greater expressions of praise, wonder and amazement in correspondence with the growing revelation of God.

> Glory to the Father, and to the Son and to
> The Holy Ghost, all paradise began:
> And the sweet song intoxicated me.
> What I saw was like a universe in smiles:
> So that intoxication came to me
> Through my vision as well as my hearing.
> O joy!  O happiness ineffable!
> O life entirely of love and peace.

Yet this also embraces the most sophisticated science, philosophy and theology of his day, repeatedly refers to the struggles of local Italian city politics and manages to underline again and again the sheer physicality of the human approach to God. In all this it preserves the human perspective of the face-to-face relationship, mainly through the growing beauty in Beatrice's face as the clarity of her vision of God increases – but finally in the face of Christ that breaks open Dante's understanding and leaves him at one with love's movement.'[18] Dante's words strike a chord in our hearts about the desire to express and experience worship that transcends our limitations and is the overflow of our souls – that lifts Christian worship to a new and sublime level. But to arrive at this deeper place of worship may not always involve a comfortable or an easy path.

Ford and Hardy point out that to reach heaven Dante had to travel through hell where God was not praised and where the atmosphere is claustrophobic, smelly, noisy, colourless and restless – the very antithesis of the constant overflow of joy in heaven.

> The Divine Comedy shows how right praise is not an optional extra in life but is the fundamental condition for happiness and for staying in harmony with reality. The claim is that the intrinsic logic of life and of Christianity are at one in this and that only in this activity are truth, beauty, goodness and love appropriately blended and fulfilled. Further by telling the story as a journey from despair to the vision of God, Dante can say a great deal about education into the many stages and levels of praise.[19]

Sotirios Christou
Cambridge November 2006

# CHAPTER ONE

## WORSHIP IN THE OLD TESTAMENT

When I was a student at theological college I was pleasantly surprised to discover from my biblical studies, that what our lecturers taught could be accessed from the books we used to write our essays. Now as an ordained minister I have found studying the Old Testament fascinating, because it means encountering the Lord through the ancient texts of our faith. Yet as a Christian I do not recall ever being gripped by any preaching on the Old Testament. David Peterson echoes a similar sentiment:

> For many Christians the Old Testament remains a mysterious and seemingly irrelevant book. At no point does it appear more distant from the needs and aspirations of people in secularised cultures than when it focuses on the temple, the sacrificial system and the priesthood. Yet these institutions were at the very heart of ancient thinking about worship and their significance must be grasped if the New Testament teaching is to be properly understood.[1]

As we explore how God instituted worship in the Old Testament this reveals a colourful drama of the theology of worship that enables us to discern what guiding principles of truth can still inform and shape our worship in the 21$^{st}$ century. And as worship is often viewed subjectively, an objective overview of the Lord's guiding principles can enable us to reflect on our pattern of worship.

### ANCIENT WORSHIP

The first instances of worship recorded in Scripture involve individuals. In Genesis 12 the Lord calls Abram to leave his country and promises to make a great nation of him and to give his descendents the land. As a response he builds an

altar to the Lord who had appeared to him – Gen. 7: 12.
Andrew Hill says: 'Abram's altar marked the site as holy
because of the Lord's appearance and demonstrated Abram's
reverence before God and his thanksgiving for the divine
word of promise.'[2]

As we read about the patriarchs in Genesis we see that
altars were a key element of their worship. Abraham built
altars at Bethel, Gen. 12: 8, Hebron, Gen. 13: 18 and at
Mount Moriah, Gen. 22: 9. Isaac built an altar at Beersheba,
Gen. 26: 25 and Jacob at Luz, Gen. 37: 7. Erecting an altar
for worship involved offering sacrifices and was also
associated with prayer. 'Altar building and the offering of
sacrifice are linked on three occasions in the patriarchal
narratives. Twice Jacob worshipped God by presenting
sacrificial offerings of an unspecified nature Gen. 31: 54, 46:
1.'[3] The most famous sacrifice in Scripture that was never
made was that of Abraham going to offer Isaac on the altar
at the command of the Lord. Hill sees this as crucial to
the development of Hebrew religion as it demonstrates
God's willingness to accommodate his revelation to cultural
conventions. He points out that human sacrifice was
practiced in ancient Mesopotamia and Abraham was no
doubt familiar with the ritual since he came from Ur of the
Chaldees – Gen. 11: 31. He also alludes to what Walter
Brueggemann calls: 'the mystery of testing and providing.'[4]

While we are aware the call from God, to sacrifice Isaac,
Abraham's only son, acts as a typology pointing to Christ
being offered for us as God's only son, this still raises
difficult questions that are not easy to answer. Although Hill
points out the Lord accommodated the cultural convention of
offering such sacrifices – this is contradicted when the Lord
rejects the golden calf as an act of worship to Him, even
though this also reflected the cultural conventions of Egypt.
Hill's assertion seems too convenient an explanation and
neatly sidesteps the controversial command to Abraham.

This request appears to be totally out of character with a loving God. Westermann says: 'Its extraordinary, frightening dimension one can only experience with empathy.'[5] Similarly, Brueggemann points out that 'it's notoriously difficult to interpret. Its difficulty begins in the aversion immediately felt for a God who will command the murder of a son.'[6] He alludes to the fact that God wants to know something. Something that God genuinely does not know. Something that is resolved in Gen. 22: 12: 'Now I know.' Now the Lord knows whether Abraham has faith to obey His command. 'We do not know why God claims the son in the first place nor finally why he will remove the demand at the end. Between the two statements of divine inscrutability stands verse 8: 'Abraham said: 'God will provide himself the lamb for a burnt offering my son.' – offering the deepest mystery of human faith and pathos.'[7] While God is omniscient he did not use his foreknowledge to know in advance Abraham's decision. That is why the test of his faith and obedience was genuinely a test and not a foregone conclusion.

The reader knows Abraham is being tested by the Lord and Isaac will be reprieved whereas Abraham is ignorant about this. Hamilton says: 'The best known event in the life of Abraham is at the same time the most baffling.'[8] He points out the divine command: 'take' is followed by the particle – *na* which is something like 'please' or 'I beg you' – is rare and only occurs five times in the O. T. when God speaks to a person. Each time God asks the individual to do something staggering. Something that defies rational explanation or understanding. Here then is an inkling that God is fully aware of the magnitude of his test for Abraham.The intensity of the test is magnified by the three distinct objects of the imperative: *your son, your precious son whom you love, Isaac...*and accentuates the solemnity of the divine imperative.'[9]

He also grasps the test for Abraham is not primarily about whether to sacrifice a beloved son although that is no doubt involved. 'The real test is whether Abraham will sacrifice the one person who can perpetuate the promises of God and particularly those promises that his posterity should thrive...Abraham appears in superhuman, somewhat unrealistic dress. He never objects to the unreasonable, slightly insane commandment to sacrifice his son. To the contrary he seems to move about his grim task with silent resignation.'[10]

Hamilton is the one who comes nearest to perceiving Abraham's unspoken confidence that God would resolve the situation when he sacrificed his son and indicates he trusted the Lord to fulfill his promises to him. Deeply engrained in his consciousness is the fact God did the impossible by giving him and Sarah a son when they were in their old age. His faith had been deeply impregnated by the truth that God could do the impossible. Abraham offering Isaac as a sacrifice only makes sense from this perspective of faith. Isaac who was born due to God's power and promise could also be raised from the dead because of God's power and promise. How else was Abraham to make sense of such an outrageous command? Without this element of unquestioning trust in the Lord his action makes no sense and is the act of a deluded man.

There is one other perspective that commentators also fail to explore – Abraham's willingness to sacrifice Isaac as an offering of worship to the Lord. If his implicit trust in the Lord to raise Isaac from the dead if he killed him is correct, he may well have understood this as an act of worship offered to the Lord. That is what offering a sacrifice on an altar to the Lord on special occasions signified – even if Abraham didn't comprehend why the Lord commanded him to do this. Matt Redman in 'Facedown' speaks about Abraham in Gen. ch. 22 as worship with a price, but this is no ordinary worship time...As they reach the appointed place and build an altar there Isaac says to his father: 'The fire and the wood are here but where is the lamb for the burnt offering?' In other words, 'Everything seems as if it's in place but where's the sacrifice?' This is always a key question when it comes to real and meaningful worship.

We would do well in our worship to ask the same question the boy Isaac asked – where is the sacrifice? Sometimes in our worship meetings the 'fire' and the 'wood' are there – in other words outwardly everything seems to be in place – and we think we're set for 'great worship.' A skilled music team perhaps, or above average songs and an enthralling preacher. But something is missing. Where is the sacrifice?'[11]

Sacrifice may be expressed in various ways in our lives. It may be seen as we give up things in order to follow Christ. Or it may be seen in our lifestyle as a Christian that Paul alludes to in Rom. 12: 1: 'I appeal to you brethren by the mercies of God, to present your bodies as a living sacrifice, holy and acceptable to God which is your spiritual worship.' Financial giving, prayer, praise and serving the Lord may all be seen as sacrifice. As Paul served the Lord and others he saw himself as 'being poured out as a libation upon the sacrificial offering of your faith' – Phil. 2: 17. Martin Selman defines sacrifice in this way – 'Once one becomes aware of the possibility that sacrifice is about the expression of a loving relationship, neither worship nor sacrifice can be confined any longer to mere action, whether performed in church or elsewhere.'[12]

In the Old Testament building an altar was also a sign a person had encountered the Lord who had spoken to him and so the place was designated a holy site. Peterson informs us: 'The great concern of people in the ancient world was to know where the presence of a god could be found and to know the names of gods so that they could be approached and communion with them established. Certain localities came to be identified as the dwelling place of the gods and here altars were erected and patterns of worship established. Part of the tradition of the shrine or the temple would be the story of how the place had come to be recognized as the abode of the god.'[13]

## THE ROOTS OF CHRISTIAN WORSHIP

The roots of Christian worship can be traced back to the spectacular saving activity of Yahweh on behalf of the Hebrews, when He rescued them in order to bring them into a covenant relationship with Him, so that he could dwell amongst them through the gift of worship. In fulfillment of His covenant to Abraham Yahweh speaks to Moses and reveals His intention to liberate the Hebrews from their bondage to the Egyptians (which lasted 450 years – Ex. 12: 40). In Ex. 3: 7, 9 the Lord had seen the affliction of His people, heard their cry because of their suffering and had come to deliver them and bring them to a land flowing with milk and honey. He made a covenant with them and gave them the gift of worship. He came to establish them as a liberated, independent nation and bring them into a land full of abundance – Ex. 3: 8, 17.

Yahweh dramatically demonstrated His power to the Hebrews through the ten plagues on Egypt, through the Passover, through the crossing of the Red Sea and through the pillar of cloud by day and fire by night that symbolised His presence with them. Moreover, when the Lord leads them to Mount Sinai His presence is accompanied by lightings and thunder – Ex. 19: 16. Here He unmistakably reveals his majesty and power to them. At mount Sinai the Lord begins to reveal His plans for His people to Moses culminating in the giving of the 10 commandments, the plans for building the ark, the tabernacle and the ordination of Aaron and his sons as priests, along with the sacrificial system and the Day of Atonement. We cannot fail to be struck by these comprehensive and elaborate details. Clearly there was nothing careless or casual in the provision of worship designed by the Lord.

## THE TABERNACLE & WORSHIP

What clearly strikes us is that all these detailed plans are divinely inspired and executed. Although God's people are invited to make freewill offerings to build the ark, the tabernacle and all the utensils in it and to make the garments for the priests, they are not invited to contribute to the Lord's design for the provision of worship. Plans for worshipping the Lord are divinely conceived. They are divinely inspired. They are carried out according to divine instructions. The central truth that informs and shapes their worship is that the Lord is holy and had to devise a means by which His people were able to be constituted holy to worship Him. Therefore, the priests and all the furniture in the tabernacle had to be consecrated to be made holy in the Lord's sight. The holiness of God points to his transcendence and that He is to be worshipped in the way He has made possible.

It is instructive to note that nearly one-third of the book of Exodus is devoted to details about the tabernacle. Here Fretheim shows acute perception when he points out that the extensiveness of the repetition in Exodus 35-40, stress the importance of obedience to the divine command concerning worship.

> ...the worship of God is not a matter in which details can be neglected. Inattention to detail may well have been a major factor in the syncretism and idolatry that developed in temple worship. A change or compromise here or there and it does not take long for worship patterns to become diverted from their original purpose and for something quite inappropriate or foreign to emerge...The forms of divine worship are not to be fundamentally a matter of human innovation or effort. And so God is not

only the architect but the giver of the specifications
for construction and the bestower of the right spirit or
inspiration for the artisans and builders. In every
conceivable way the tabernacle and its associated
worship must be built according to the will of God.[14]

Motyer also says: 'the tabernacle could make a strong bid
to be the greatest of all biblical visual aids…and it would be
allowable to say that there cannot be a single detail of the
tabernacle devoid of any meaning.'[15] He provides a detailed
explanation of the significance of the tabernacle, the ark and
all the other ceremonial objects, along with the robes which
Aaron and his sons as priests had to wear every day. He
also explains the meaning of all the different sacrifices the
priests had to make which culminated in the Day of
Atonement. At first sight only a preacher or a theologian
would choose to study these things as they do not appear
relevant for worship today, especially as they have been
made obsolete by the atoning death of Christ. So it is not
surprising if Christians find more interesting topics about
worship to focus on than the book of Exodus. Yet it contains
truths that can shape our worship today.

## GOD'S PRESENCE
Studying the roots of Christian worship from the book
of Exodus reminds us that God's desire is to dwell with His
people. As a sign confirming this He bound himself to them
in a covenant relationship and gave them the gift of worship.
So God revealed himself through His saving activity,
by speaking to His people on Mount Sinai through Moses
and by giving them the gift of the law. For God's presence to
remain with them and for the Lord to remain in relationship
with His people, sacrifices had to offered up every morning
and evening. This is a clear reminder of God's holiness and
the separation that existed between Him and His people. The
Lord's appearance on Mount Sinai and the thunder and
smoke that accompanied this were signs of His glory, His

majesty and His transcendence. Here we are struck by the 'otherness' of God. By His 'numinous character' and that he is unapproachable. We are clearly dealing with the 'sacred' when contemplating God in Exodus. The otherness of God is something Matt Redman touches upon when he says: 'For worship to be worship, it must contain something of the otherness of God.'[16]

## HOLY – HOLY – HOLY

When we read how all the furniture and vessels in the tabernacle and the priests involved in worship had to be consecrated, either with blood or anointing oil to be made holy, this highlights the truth that only by being constituted holy can God's people have access to worship Him. We do not know how long the Lord took to conceive the gift of worship, but we do know that it involved elaborate details. It involved painstaking care in building the tabernacle and the ark and ordaining the priests. It involved care in offering daily sacrifices of worship acceptable to the Lord. The focus on the holiness of the Lord and the necessity of consecrating everything and everyone involved in worship, so that they too were constituted holy, finds its fullest expression in the ark in the holy of holies in the tabernacle. Motyer highlights this emphasis when he says:

> The ark represented the Lord in his unapproachable holiness. It was the sole piece of furniture in the innermost shrine with not even a stand to support it. As a box it contained the stone tablets of the law which stated in ten precepts both what the Lord is like in his holiness and what he requires his people to be (holy). As such the ark exposed the sins and shortcomings of those the Lord had redeemed by contrasting what he in his moral distinctiveness is like, with what they in their moral weaknesses are like. It was a physical reminder of why God lives in isolation and why his people cannot enter his presence.[17]

At first glance the contemporary relevance of dedicating
the furniture in the tabernacle used in worship so that it is
symbolically holy in the Lord's eyes – may not be obvious
and easily overlooked. This may be the case when the
sanctuary-stage where worship is conducted has been taken
over by modern technology, sound equipment and the band.
The tabernacle sets the precedent of dedicating everything
used in worship so that it is constituted holy to the Lord.
This would ensure that all the musical instruments on the
sanctuary-stage are dedicated to God so they are consecrated
holy in our worship. The sanctuary can also be a reminder of
drawing near to the holy of holies – into the very presence
of God. To what extent should the sanctuary-stage where
worship is led visually remind us that symbolically this is a
'sacred space?' Is it time for the Lord to be the central focus
of this area by giving this space back to Him, and moving all
the musicians and sound technology so they do not dominate
this 'sacred space?'

The Lord's gift of the 10 commandments to His people
written on two tablets of stone and placed in the ark were
a reminder of God's holy character. Not only did God
command obedience to His instructions in building the
tabernacle and all its component parts, he commanded
obedience in keeping the law and the commandments. We do
the Lord a great disservice if we interpret this request in a
legalistic way. Fretheim says: 'It is not obedience vis-à-vis
an objective law code obeying the law for the sake of the
law. *It is obedience to the one who gives the law.* It is to
keep God himself and loyalty and allegiance to this God as
the focus of their sheer attention in these matters. That is
why the law initially comes as direct divine address to the
people: to keep the law orientated in terms of personal
relationship. The law given by God to Israel is in effect a
laying down of the expectations for the relationship. It is the
means for Israel to know what being faithful to God entails
in the living out of life within the relationship. For God to

have expectations for the relationship with Israel at all is to acknowledge that these constitute a test.'[18]

## THE GLORY OF THE LORD

In Exodus 40 the Lord told Moses to erect the tabernacle and gave him the instructions to do this. As all the component parts were assembled and all the furniture put in place, the Lord instructed him to anoint the tabernacle and everything in it with the anointing oil they had made. He also told him to wash Aaron and his sons with water and put on their holy garments as priests and to anoint them – Ex. 40: 1-15. After carrying out all the Lord's instructions we learn in v. 34 that the cloud then covered the tent of meeting and the glory of the Lord filled the tabernacle. And Moses was not able to enter the tent of meeting because of the cloud upon it and the glory of the Lord filled the tabernacle.

> When all is ready, God comes to dwell among the people in the completed tabernacle. The sanctuary is not simply a symbol of the divine presence – *it is an actual vehicle for divine immanence,* in and through which the transcendent God dwells. The concern for consecration and an appropriate setting for the Holy One makes it clear that the *tabernacle does not collapse presence into immanence.* The God who is present is present as the transcendent one. It is as the Holy One that God is present.[19]

Similarly when Solomon had dedicated the Temple and the holy vessels were placed in it, as they were praising the Lord – His glory filled the Temple and the priests could not stand in the presence of the Lord to minister – 2 Chron. 5: 14. Moreover, when Solomon prayed after dedicating the Temple once again the glory of the Lord descended. Again the priests could not enter because of the cloud of the glory of the Lord – 2 Chron. 7: 2

As we reflect upon the Lord's detailed plans for the tabernacle and also for the Temple, we cannot fail to be struck by the attention to detail and the care that was required to build them. What also stands out is the holiness of God and His unapproachable presence that manifested itself in His glory in the sanctuary. So overwhelming was the holiness and presence of the Lord that the priests literally could not enter. As we reflect on these truths this is a reminder of the care required in coming to worship the Lord. In Exodus and 2 Chronicles the glory of the Lord militates against coming casually or thoughtlessly to worship Him. These passages also present us with the ultimate climax of Christian worship – the manifestation of the presence and glory of the Lord in an overwhelming way.

## THE FEAR OF THE LORD

One of the characteristics of contemporary worship is its informality. In this setting ministers may not wear robes and in some instances do not even wear a clerical collar and the congregation also dress casually or informally. Any traditional liturgy has probably been dispensed with and in some churches an entertainment culture almost pervades the manner in which parts of the service are conducted.

This informality may intentional aim to reflect the intimacy in relationship with the Lord that this spirituality espouses. In contrast to many traditional churches where the emphasis on knowing the Lord in an intimate way is rarely highlighted, this is a real strength of this style of worship. Alongside this there are obvious dangers in this approach. Informality can almost inadvertently assume an unhealthy familiarity, that reflects a lack of reverence in our approach to worshipping the Lord. This can result in an insidious complacency that deceives people into thinking their worship has arrived and 'really rocks.'

Regardless of our style of worship how exactly is the fear of the Lord to be expressed in our Services? In Exodus and Deuteronomy we come across the term 'the fear of the Lord' in Israel's relationship with God. His people are to fear the Lord and this is found in the context of keeping His commandments. The knowledge of God's law is intended to affect their response to the Lord, so that their lives reflect a reverence towards Him by living within the bounds he has set. This can be described in terms of personal piety and devotion to the Lord. Hill says: 'This fearful reverence for God Almighty motivated both worship and service on the part of   the righteous according to the O. T. – Deut. 6:13, 10: 20.' It 'was religious devotion in the richest sense of the phrase – and a reverence for God which expresses itself in positive responses to God and His word…The fear of the Lord is an attitude that includes the emotion of reverence and awe for a unique, holy, all powerful, all-knowing God. It is primarily a way of life based on a sober estimate of God's presence and care. This fear of the Lord fostered an awareness among the Hebrew faithful that God is clearly above all, providentially ensuring the outcome of a personal life in accordance with one's character and action…Only the fear of Yahweh preserves the inscrutable nature of God and maintains the profound mystery of life.'[20]

Darlene Zscech's definition of the fear of the Lord adds another dimension for consideration:

> The fear of the Lord is a deep, reverential
> sense of our accountability to Him.[21]

This is a disposition of the heart we bring when we come to worship the Lord. Our fear of the Lord will also have an impact on the way we approach our worship and the manner in which we conduct it – regardless of whether our style is traditional or contemporary. And the ethos of our worship can express our reverence for and our fear of the Lord. All that we do and the way we do it will be motivated by our desire to honour the Lord. In such an atmosphere of worship I would go as far as to say, the fear of the Lord will have an evangelistic impact on any non-believers who are present.

## RELIGIOUS FESTIVALS

Just as we have seasons in the liturgical calendar such as Advent, Christmas, Easter and Pentecost, Israel also had a rich tradition of festivals the Lord provided for them. These were incorporated into the festival liturgies of the Hebrew religious calendar. Seven major festivals were observed in New Testament times. 'For the most part these festivals were connected to the important historical events of early Israelite history. The specific ritual re-enactments associated with each festival not only dramatised Hebrew history but also evoked memories of God and His covenant relationship with Israel. This liturgical symbolism was employed for the theological education of the religious community in the divine works of deliverance and redemption.'[22]

* The Feast of Booths or Tabernacles associated with the wilderness wanderings after the Exodus was a reminder of Israel's temporary homes during her time in the wilderness (Lev. 23: 33-43).
* The Feast of Trumpets, later known as Rosh Hashanah or 'New Year' when the blowing of the ceremonial trumpet marked the beginning of the new religious year (Lev. 23: 24-25).
* The Feast of Purim celebrates the deliverance of the Hebrews by Esther the Queen under Xerxes the King in Persia (Esther 3: 27, 9: 20-32).
* The Feast of Dedication or Lights (John 10: 22-29) commemorates the cleansing and dedication of the second temple in 164 BC. It is known as Hannukah and was marked by the lighting of candles for eight days. This symbolised the divine light of God's revealed word to His people (Psalm 27: 1, 36: 9, 119: 105).

* The Feast of Unleavened Bread and Passover are the first of the major feasts in the religious calendar and historically and theologically the most important (Lev. 23: 4-5). The Passover was a family meal with the sacrifice of the lamb which re-enacted deliverance from Egypt, during which children were invited to ask questions about the meaning of this festival. The seven day feast of Unleavened Bread linked the Passover and was a reminder of the years of sorrow and bitterness in bondage in Egypt.

* The Feast of Weeks or Pentecost was also called the Feast of the Harvest or Day of first-fruits and celebrated the end of the barley harvest (Ex. 23: 6). This festival was also called Pentecost (*pente* meaning fifty) because it came fifty days after the barley harvest and was a time of great rejoicing before the Lord and a time for bringing freewill offerings to Him for the harvest.

* The Day of Atonement or Yom Kippur (Lev. 16) was the national day of repentance and sacrifice for sin in ancient Israel. Once a year on this day the high priest entered the Holy of Holies to make atonement for the sins of all the people.Of special significance was the symbolic transference of community sin to the head of the scapegoat which was led off into the wilderness. A typology of the substitutionary character of Hebrew worship which prophetically pointed to Christ. In contrast to other joyful religious festivals this was a day of mourning and sorrow.

Important truths may be learnt from these Hebrew religious festivals. 'First, God ordered Jewish worship in such a way that there were cycles of exciting worship celebrations at regular intervals during the year. Second, these festivals connected the worship of God with concrete historical events on the part of Yahweh for His people. Third, joyous celebration was balanced with sober reflection. And fourth the festivals offered a variety of participatory worship experiences...The festivals were elaborate. They were demanding. They were joyous for the most part and they were interesting.'[23]

## MOUNT SINAI

In the book of Exodus as we read about the plagues, the Hebrews' escape from Egypt, the miraculous crossing of the Red Sea, the Lord appearing on Mount Sinai and speaking to them and giving detailed instructions for the building of the tabernacle and the elaborate ordination of Aaron and his sons as priests by Moses – we might well think we have entered the fictional world of the big screen movie block buster of Cecil B. DeMilles' film The Ten Commandments. He rightly saw this as a spectacular movie with God as the central character and leading protagonist. It is a story set in an alien culture far removed from us. It is an ancient tale of God who has begun to reveal himself and come to dwell amongst His people. It is a record of elaborate rituals and blood stained sacrifices that result in the worship of Yahweh. At first glance Exodus does not appear to make scintillating reading – but as we approach these ancient rituals with reverence, we discover the origin and typology of Christian worship that found its ultimate fulfillment in Christ.

Moses has been on Mount Sinai with the Lord forty days and nights and meanwhile the Hebrews are getting restless. They are bored and frustrated with waiting for him to return. Despite the Lord working mighty miracles through Moses the people are not overly impressed with him. In fact they are somewhat dismissive – 'When the people saw that Moses had delayed to come down from the mountain, the people gathered themselves together to Aaron and said to him: 'Up make gods for us, who shall go before us: as for this Moses, this man who brought us out of Egypt, we do not know what has become of him' – Ex. 32: 1. B. Childs says: 'There is a certain note of threat in the choice of the verb to describe the peoples' initial approach to Aaron...' and 'The abusive reference to Moses with flippant unconcern sets the tone for the coming activity.'[24]

The miracles the Lord performed, the covenant to be their God and the words He spoke at Mount Sinai, introduced them to revolutionary salvation theology. There is nothing to compare this activity of God as He revealed himself with any religious belief system they previously held. Meanwhile all that Moses asked of them was to wait for him to come down from Mount Sinai – Ex. 24: 14. What was asked and required of them was to trust the Lord to show them the way ahead for the future. But they didn't trust. And they didn't wait.

## THE SPIRIT OF THE AGE

The Lord knew the provision for worship He was going to reveal to them through Moses. Meanwhile, back on the mountain, the Hebrews didn't know the Lord was giving Moses precise details about worship, concerning building the tabernacle and the Holy of Holies, and instructions about the sacrificial system and the ordination of Aaron and his sons as priests. The Lord was making preparations to dwell amongst them through the provision of worship.

As the people took matters into their own hands Aaron capitulated to their demand by forging a golden calf that reflected the gods-idols in Egypt. This was tantamount to 'uninformed worship' impregnated with secular idolatry that reflected the spirit of their age. Some commentators think there may be a certain ambiguity in interpreting this scene, although what they do is explicit enough. Was the calf a substitute messenger for Moses who had gone absent? Was it a symbol to represent the Lord going with them? Was it a casual act to replicate an image of a calf as a cultural symbol from Egypt? Fretheim sees a deeper, more calculated significance that the Hebrews may have attached to this image. He perceives that the phrase 'go before' in

connection with the calf is used only of God's messenger
in Exodus, which suggests the people are requesting an
image of the messenger of God. In this way they make
the representation concrete and accessible, having a greater
independence from Yahweh. The construction of an image
of the divine messenger would give that figure a more
permanent place at the lead of the community, no longer
dependent on Moses' mediation.[25]

The golden calf shows that the Hebrews had been deeply
influenced by the prevailing spirit of idolatry that pervaded
their stay in Egypt. They had assimilated this cultural icon
they had been exposed to. Aaron goes along with the people
in making the idol presumably because he thought it was
an acceptable way of celebrating their deliverance and
worshipping the Lord. The people said: 'These are your gods
O Israel, who brought you up out of the land of Egypt!
When Aaron saw this he built an altar before it: and Aaron
made proclamation and said: 'Tomorrow shall be a feast to
the Lord.' And they rose up early on the morrow and offered
burnt offerings and brought peace offerings: and the people
sat down to eat and drink and rose up to play' – Ex. 32: 4-6.
Childs appears to be somewhat generous in exonerating
Aaron in this incident when he says: 'Obviously Aaron had
had a different intention from the people when he made the
calf. The fact that he could incorporate the calf in a Yahweh
festival indicates that he did not understand it as blatant
apostasy from Yahweh.'[26] But he then contradicts himself
when he says:

> The people have corrupted themselves. If in the
> instructions of God to Moses one can see the true
> will of God for Israel's worship, in the golden calf
> one can also see the perversion of worship...the
> alternative worship to true worship is held up as a
> terrifying threat which undercuts the very ground of
> Israel's existence.[27]

It is difficult to see how one can extricate Aaron from his complicity in the golden calf incident, seeing he actually was the one who made it.

## UNINFORMED WORSHIP

Whether deliberately or inadvertently the Hebrews made a catastrophic error of judgment as the cultural assimilation of the golden calf in their worship was idolatrous and unacceptable to the Lord. The calf represented much more than a visual aid. The underlying issues involved not trusting the Lord, rejecting Him and being unfaithful to the covenant He recently made with them. Moreover, they were breaking the first three commandments in Ex. 20. This incident illustrates the polluted worship God's people offered to the Lord when acting on their own initiative. Their ignorance of the Lord's provision for worship stands in stark contrast to their idolatrous calf. Fretheim draws a damning comparison between the worship the Hebrews initiated and the worship the Lord had planned for them.

> In every key point the peoples' building project contrasts with the tabernacle that God has just announced. The people seek to create what God had already provided. They rather than God take the initiative. Offerings are demanded rather than willingly presented. The elaborate preparations are missing altogether. The painstaking length of time needed for building becomes an overnight rush job. The careful provision for guarding the presence of the Holy One turns into an open-air object of immediate accessibility. The invisible, intangible God becomes a visible, tangible image. The personal, active God becomes an impersonal object that cannot see or speak or act.The ironic effect is that the people forfeit the very divine presence they had hoped to bind more closely to themselves.[28]

The Hebrews' worship is crude, rudimentary and tainted by the spirit of idolatry they had assimilated from Egypt. As yet they did not understand the implications of their sin and God's holiness: and that worship could only be offered to God on His terms rather than by humanly instituted sacrifices that reflected the prevailing, sinful culture of their day.

In our generation God's people would be prudent to take care as they seek to be culturally relevant in their worship. Are they embracing practices in their contemporary worship they consider to be acceptable, while failing to realise they may have capitulated to the prevailing spirits of our age? What God's people may consider acceptable in their worship may in fact be counterfeit, idolatrous and unacceptable to the Lord.

## THE GIFT OF PRIESTHOOD

In the Old Testament to understand the theology about priesthood you have to start with God – who took the initiative to instigate the sacrificial system and the priesthood after He delivered the Hebrews from bondage in Egypt and drew them into a covenant relationship with himself. The tabernacle, the ark and the priesthood, along with the sacrificial system and the commandments were all a gift and a sign of God's grace.

The tabernacle acted as a perpetual reminder of God's presence with His people and the priestly sacrifices were also a reminder of God's holiness. Sacrifice as a gift enabled atonement for sin to take place as God had decreed. Therefore, God could dwell in the tabernacle in the Holy of Holies in the midst of His people. Concerning priesthood and sacrifice Gordon Wenham says: 'At the heart of this scheme was the establishment of a pure system of worship, in which God could be honoured and praised in a fitting manner and through which human sin could be atoned for.'[29] This highlights another important aspect of the sacrificial system

– the offering to God of acceptable worship. Worship was the calling of Israel when God delivered them from Egypt, as we see from Ex. 3: 18–19. Worship according to the pattern God was going to give to His people.

## THE DAY OF ATONEMENT

The Day of Atonement is intimately associated with the priesthood and involves a focus on blood as this was integral to the sacrificial system. To understand the significance of blood helps to clarify that sacrifices in the Old Testament acted as a typology for the sacrifice of Christ shedding his blood. Wenham says:

> Under the law almost everything is purified with blood and without the shedding of blood there is no forgiveness of sins (Heb. 9: 22).[30]

And in Leviticus the shedding of blood is associated with cleansing and sanctification.

> All these sacrifices involved the shedding of blood and all these sacrifices reached their annual climax on the Day of Atonement. On this day each part of the tabernacle was smeared with blood.[31]

This is a reminder that the purification of the sanctuary is central to this special day, along with he purification of the people from their sins.

Entry into the Most Holy Place, the Holy of Holies, where the ark of the covenant was placed was only allowed once a year on the Day of Atonement and only after elaborate preparation by the high priest. The ark was the visible symbol of the presence and glory of God and Lev. 16 outlines the preparation of the high priest and the people for this special day. Bellinger says: 'The priest functions as the mediator between the people and God and as we have seen before, he must be properly prepared for that role especially here where encounter with the divine presence is so intense.'[32]

The Day of Atonement was a special day in the life of
Israel and before Aaron offered a sacrifice for the sin of the
nation, he had to make a sin offering for himself and for his
household – then the Holy of Holies itself had to be cleansed
too. Aaron had to sacrifice a bull as a sin offering for himself
and enter the Holy of Holies with a censer full of coals from
the altar before the Lord, with two handfuls of incense
beaten small and bring it within the veil and put the incense
on the fire before the Lord – so the cloud of the incense
covered the mercy seat which is upon the testimony, lest he
die by being exposed to God's glory in the Holy of Holies.
Then he had to take some of the bull's blood and sprinkle it
with his finger on the front of the mercy seat and before the
mercy seat, and sprinkle the blood with his finger seven
times – Lev. 16: 11-14.This highlights the truth that in God's
eyes: 'The blood rites purify the Most Holy Place from any
defilement.'[33]

Aaron then had to kill the goat of the sin offering for the
people, bring its blood within the veil and sprinkle its blood
on the mercy seat on top of the ark and before the mercy
seat. In this way he made atonement for the holy place
because of the uncleanesses of the people of Israel and
because of their transgressions. He also had to do the same
for the tent of meeting. He then had to cleanse the altar
before the Lord also with the blood of the bull and the blood
of the goat by sprinkling it on the horns of the altar – Lev.
16: 15-19. Blood cleansed the altar as well as consecrating it.
'The blood rite to purify the sanctuary enables the divine
presence to continue in the midst of the community. Thus the
divine-human relationship is back at 'one' for Aaron, the
other priests, and the community.'[34]

With the purification of the holy place complete we now
have the third major element in the ritual on the Day
of Atonement – the scapegoat. When Aaron had finished
making atonement for these things he had to present a live

goat in the Holy of Holies, and lay both his hands on the
head of the goat and cover over him all the sin of the people
of Israel. Then he presented the goat to the people and sent
him away into the wilderness with a man ready to take him
there – Lev. 16: 20-22. The goat was symbolically taking the
sin of the nation away into the wilderness. This was a sign
that God had put away the sin of His people. Bellinger says:
'The goat carries the sins to a solitary place far from the
community and far from the divine dwelling place. The goat
is then released in a place from which it is unlikely to return.
The sins thus cannot threaten the holiness in the midst of the
camp, and so can no longer bring damage to ancient Israel.'[35]

On the Day of Atonement the people (all the nation) also
had their duty and responsibility as we see from Lev. 16: 29:
'And it shall be a statute (a permanent rule) that you must
afflict yourselves and not do any work.' Preparation for this
special day has connotations of penitence probably involving
prayer and self-examination. Ultimately, however impressive
though the ceremonies were which were carried out by the
high priest, on their own they were insufficient. If they were
to be effective the nation had to demonstrate true penitence.
Reflecting on the sacrificial system of Israel Jenson says:

> The tabernacle and its sacrificial system is thus a
> gracious gift from God which allows a liberated
> people to worship and serve God in holiness.[36]

# CHAPTER TWO

# COUNTERFEIT WORSHIP

## INTRODUCTION

As we read the prophetic books in the Old Testament it may be difficult to grasp how Israel succumbed to the temptation to worship idols of wood and stone instead of the Lord. It may seem incomprehensible to us how these pagan practices infiltrated the worship of the Temple – but the perennial temptation facing God's people is to become so familiar with the cultural practices of their day, that they assimilate them and inadvertently become part of the ethos of Christian worship. Jeremiah and his famous Temple sermon and the background leading up to this, illustrates how this happened and what the Lord had to say about it.

From Jeremiah's priestly background he would have been familiar with the tradition of the law and the Sinai Covenant between Yahweh and Israel. He would have known that obedience and faithfulness to the Lord resulted in blessing, but failure resulted in judgment and the curse of the law – Deut. 30:1-20. He spoke about the covenant relationship between the Lord and Israel as a marriage commitment and pointing to Israel's failure to keep the covenant he described this as adultery and harlotry (see ch. 2-3). Now the historical background of the covenant occupies a central role in understanding Jeremiah.

Jeremiah was a symbolic preacher and at times used visual aids to proclaim his message. One that contained repeated warnings to Israel to repent along with the threat of judgment if the nation failed to respond. His message of judgment was due to Israel's apostasy as she abandoned her allegiance to the Lord and her love for Him. His ministry began in the reign of Josiah around 625 BC and spanned forty turbulent years. This continued throughout the reign of Jehoiakim, Josiah's son and until the 11th year of Zedekiah son of Josiah, until the captivity of Jerusalem in the fifth month – Jer. 1: 1-4. To appreciate the situation in Josiah's day when Jeremiah's ministry began it is helpful to know Josiah's background. His grandfather Manasseh did not walk in the ways of the Lord. He allowed all kinds of pagan religious practices that were idolatrous and broke Israel's covenant commitment with the Lord. He also tolerated prostitution in the Temple area – 2 kings 21 the worship of Baal, the erection of an Asherah – a statue of a pagan god to be worshipped and the worship of astral gods and a host of other abominations. Clearly authentic worship of the Lord as he had decreed was perverted beyond all recognition.

Josiah's father Amnon also continued in these evil ways during his reign – 2 kings 21. However, when Josiah became king, as a young man he began to seek the Lord and to walk in his ways – 2 Chron. 34: 1-3. He sought to bring about religious reforms and purge the land of pagan practices. During this time the temple was repaired – 2 Kings 22 and the Book of the Law was found.

## JEREMIAH & IDOLATROUS WORSHIP

The second chapter of Jeremiah is one of the most moving and tragic chapters in Scripture and the powerful impact it has is two fold. Firstly, the Lord reveals his deepest love for his people and like a spurned lover he pours out his heart at the loss of his loved one Israel. There is a beauty and a magnetic quality about God's unfettered love that he declares to his people. Secondly, the other piercing impact is the great sadness we glimpse at Judah's and Israel's apostasy that resulted in idolatrous worship and ultimately led to God's judgment. In response to their apostasy the Lord declares his love for his people through Jeremiah, to call them to repent and return to their first love for him. Tragically this was unreciprocated. We perceive a great sense of loss as the Lord is heartbroken by his peoples' failure to love him andworship him

The structure and style of chapter 2 is like a court case in which the Lord brings charges against Israel and Judah. He does this by asking them questions. The main charge that the Lord brings against his people is that of apostasy. Apostasy means that Judah and Israel have changed their God, the Lord. They have forsaken him and no longer give him their allegiance or worship. Instead they give their love and worship to other gods, the Canaanite gods and the Baals.

As in a court case the Lord asks his people certain questions: 'What wrong did your fathers find in me that they went far from me?'– 2: 5. 'For cross to the coasts of Cyprus and see or send to Kedar and examine with care see if there has been such a thing. Has a nation changed its gods even though they are no gods? But my people have changed their glory for that which does not profit'– 2: 10-11. The people have rejected the Lord and their sin of idolatry is so serious it profoundly angers the Lord and is detestable to him. In 2: 12-13 there is strong emotive language to describe the impact this has on the Lord. 'Be appalled O heavens, be shocked be utterly desolate, for my people have committed two evils. They have forsaken me the fountain of living waters and hewn out cisterns for themselves that can hold no water.' Brueggemann says:

> But Israel in its recalcitrance exchanges the only true God for the gods of Canaan who cannot profit. Israel has distorted things at the foundation not being able to sort out what is real and unreal, what is true and false, what is life giving and death dealing.[1]

The deceptive nature of worshipping idols leads to their delusion. This is so insidious that what is real becomes false and what is false assumes reality. As a result God's people were not only deluded but blinded to the true nature of their action. Adam Welch suggests that Israel trades gods because this one is too demanding. He is on to something here. Worshipping a domesticated idol makes no demands on the worshippers.

> There was no cause to forsake such gods because it involved so little to follow them. Israel forsook Yahweh because the relation to Him was full of ethical content. Yahwism had this iron core in it. The iron core was that Israel could only have Yahweh on his terms.Yahwism was no colourless faith which was simply the expression of people's pride in itself and in its destiny. It laid a curb on men. It had a yoke and bonds. The bonds were those of love: but love's bonds are the most enduring and the most exacting.[2]

Ch.2: 4-37 divides into five sections and verse four sums up what happened to God's people: 'They went far from the Lord' – because they turned to idols and failed to worship him. There are four key words in these verses.

In   4 - 8   key word - FAITHLESS to the Lord.
In   9 -13   key word - FORSAKEN the Lord.
In  14 -28   key word - FEARLESS no fear of the Lord.
In  29 -32   key word - FORGOTTEN the Lord.

Faithless – forsaken – fearless – forgotten: these are the four subsidiary charges the Lord brings against Israel as in a court case. In verse 5 we have the first charge – the people were faithless and went after worthless idols and became worthless themselves. In verse 6 they forgot the Lord's past faithfulness and they forgot to seek the Lord too. They defiled and polluted the land through idol worship. We also see from verse 7 Israel and Judah became an abomination to the Lord.

* In v. 8 four classes of rulers are charged with being faithless. The priests are charged with not seeking the Lord. The Levites the teachers of the law are charged with not

knowing God. The political leaders are charged with sinning against the Lord. The prophets are charged with prophesying by baal.

* In v. 9-13 the Lord continues with his charges and contends with his people and challenges them about their idolatrous behaviour. They have gone after Canaanite gods of wood and stone and deflected their worship from the living God.

* In v. 10-11 the Lord confronts his people as they have changed gods. Their behaviour is unparalleled and un-precedented. It is also unheard of. Even pagan nations do not change their gods even though they are non-existent.

* In v. 11 the Lord says: 'But my people have changed the glory of knowing me, for that which does not profit.' In v. 12 the heavens are called to act as witnesses to this court trial that God has instigated against his people.

The Lord speaks passionately as he describes his peoples' idolatry and the serious nature of their sin. It not an exaggeration to say when the Lord sees his people giving their devotion, their love and worship to other gods and idols it is a horrendous sin in his sight. The idolatry of Israel and Judah was detestable to the Lord. In verse 13 the Lord points out the unthinkable. His people have forsaken him the fountain of living water and hewn out cisterns for themselves that can hold no water. In other words they made idols with their own hands that have no spiritual life and worship them. In God's eyes this was astonishing behaviour and resulted in his judgment on his people.

It is appropriate to ask: 'What has their idolatry done to the people and how has it affected them?' The first striking impression we glimpse from Jer. ch. 2 is the way the people see themselves.

V. 20 'I will not serve.' They rebelled against the Lord.

V. 23 'I am not defiled.' The people have been deceived.

V. 27 But in time of trouble they say – 'Arise save us.'

Yet their faith had no foundation it was false.
They had been deluded by their idolatry.

V. 31 'We are free we will come to you no more.'
The people had become rebellious.

V. 35 'I am innocent, surely his anger has turned from me?'
The people who were deceived by their idolatry had
a false perception of their relationship with Lord.

The second revealing insight we glimpse from Jer. Ch.
2 is the contrast in the way the Lord sees his people.

V. 5 They went after worthless idols and became
worthless in the process.

V. 7 They have defiled the land through their idolatry.

V. 14 They have become a slave and prey to foreign nations.

V. 20 They bowed down as a harlot to idols in high places.

V. 22 The stain of your guilt is before me.

V. 27 They said to a tree: 'You are my father.'
And to a stone: 'You gave me birth.'

V. 29 'Why do you complain against me?'
They complained because the Lord didn't help them.
Blinded by their sin they failed to grasp this.

V. 30 They ignored the Lord's discipline. Therefore
because of these things the Lord says: 'Behold I will
bring you to judgment for saying: 'I have not sinned.'

V. 39 The Lord has been heartbroken by his peoples'
idolatry. In contrast they have been totally blind and ignorant
of what they have done. This is the result of their idolatrous
behaviour,that utterly deceived them and led to false worship.

Jer. ch. 2 is not only very moving and tragic it is also very
disturbing. Disturbing because God's people were unaware
of how worshipping idols had affected them. In verse 32 the
Lord says:

Can a maiden forget her ornaments, or a bride her
attire? Yet my people have forgotten me days
without number.

God's people could not see how their idolatry had affected
them and their relationship with the Lord. As a result under
the terms of the covenant in Exodus they have brought
judgment upon themselves. Jeremiah's preaching was an
attempt to appeal to Judah's and Israel's imagination. He
required courage to confront the reality of their idolatrous
world view that they had constructed. Brueggemann says:

> The convergence of religious fickleness, political
> whoredom and covenantal disregard shows that
> Jeremiah is engaged in an acute critical analysis…
> He struggles here as frequently with the incredible
> obtuseness of this people. Not only is there an
> abandonment ofGod but covenantal sensitivities have
> so collapsed that Israel is unable to recognize the
> quality and shape of its actions. In the face of the data
> so clear to Jeremiah Judah continues to maintain
> innocence.[3]

Jeremiah ch. 2 presents us with three searching questions.
Firstly, what idols have we inadvertently welcomed into our
lives, or what idols have gained access into our lives by our
deliberate sin? We are challenged to ask the Holy Spirit to
search our hearts and lives, to reveal any idols we have
become blind to–that we may  repent of them and evict them.

Secondly, what idols have insidiously gained entrance into
our church life and our traditional or contemporary worship?
Has our spirituality or worship become an idol? We are
challenged to ask the Lord by his Spirit to show us where
any idols have infiltrated our worship that we are blind to,
that we may repent of them and evict them.

Thirdly, how might Jeremiah ch. 2 apply to us as a nation?
What comparison can we see between the idolatrous worship
of Israel and Judah and our nation? Have we also become
blind and deceived by the idols our nation has erected

and worships?  Over the past 30 years there has been much talk of spiritual renewal, but the question Jeremiah leaves us with is a very disturbing one. He forces us to ask ourselves the most unpalatable question – 'Are we as a nation under God's judgment – because we have failed to worship Him?'

## UNACCEPTABLE WORSHIP

Israel's religious practice is the background to the serious indictment of Jeremiah's temple sermon concerning their unacceptable worship. Ch. 7 records this sermon and ch. 26 the response to it. It is helpful to have these passages before us as we consider the issue of unacceptable worship. The word that came to Jeremiah from the Lord in ch. 7: 1-15:

> Stand in the gate of the Lord's house and proclaim there this word and say: Hear the word of the Lord all you men of Judah who enter these gates to worship the Lord. Thus says the Lord of hosts the God of Israel amend your ways and your doings and I will let you dwell in this place. Do not trust in these deceptive words: 'This is the temple of the Lord, the temple of the Lord, the temple of the Lord.'

> Behold you trust in deceptive words to no avail. Will you steal, murder, commit adultery, swear falsely, burn incense to Baal and go after other gods you have not known – and then come and stand before me in this house which is called by my name and say: 'We are delivered!'– only to go on doing all these abominations? Has this house which is called by my name become a den of robbers in your eyes?  Behold I myself have seen it says the Lord. Go now to my place that was in Shiloh where I made my name dwell at first and see what I did to it for the wickedness of my people Israel. And now because you have done all these things says the Lord, and when I spoke to you persistently you did not listen, and when I called you

did not answer, therefore I will do to the house which
is called by my name and in which you trust, and to
the place which I gave you and to your fathers as I did
to Shiloh. And I will cast you out of my sight as I cast
out all your kinsmen, all the offspring of Ephraim.

We see the response to Jeremiah's sermon in 26: 7-16, 24.
The priests, the prophets and all the people heard Jeremiah
and these words in the house of the Lord. And when he had
finished speaking all that the Lord had commanded him
to speak to all the people, then the priests and the prophets
and all the people laid hold of him saying: 'You shall die!
Why have you prophesied in the name of the Lord saying:
'This house shall be like Shiloh and this city shall be desolate
without inhabitants?' And all the people gathered about
Jeremiah in the house of the Lord. When the princes of Judah
heard these things they came up from the King's house to the
house of the Lord and took their seat in the entry of the New
Gate of the house of the Lord. Then the priests and the
prophets said to the princes and to all the people: 'This man
deserves the sentence of death because he has prophesied
against this city as you have heard with your own ears.' Then
Jeremiah spoke to all the princes and the people saying: 'The
Lord sent me to prophecy against this house and this city all
the words you have heard. Now therefore amend your ways
and your doings and obey the voice of the Lord your God
and the Lord will repent of the evil which he has pronounced
against you. But as for me behold I am in your hands. Do
with me as seems good and right to you. Only know for
certain that if you put me to death you will bring innocent
blood upon yourselves and this city and its inhabitants, for in
truth the Lord sent me to you to speak all these words in your
ears.' Then the princes and all the people said to the priests
and the prophets: 'This man does not deserve the sentence of
death for he has spoken to us in the name of the Lord our
God.'…But the hand of Ahikam the son of Shapan was with

Jeremiah so that he was not given over to the peoples to be put to death.

## FALSE CONFIDENCE IN WORSHIP

In Jeremiah's day the political and religious leaders believed Israel was secure as a nation because they were God's covenant people. Their prevailing conviction was that Jerusalem was inviolable (completely secure from her enemies) because of God's unconditional promises. This was the religious philosophy that under-girded their national life and gave them a sense of security. They echoed this in the confident declaration: 'the temple of the Lord.' Their belief that the protection of the Lord was guaranteed was the foundation that underpinned the political and religious establishment. But the Lord called Jeremiah to challenge and refute this false temple ideology.

In his temple sermon Jeremiah challenged the temple worship along with the false confidence and trust the people associated with the temple theology. They blindly and tenaciously held on to their national religious heritage and clung to a corporate belief about God's divine favour as his chosen people. Sadly, this public liturgical formula – 'the temple of the Lord' was not substantiated by observing the Lord's commands. Into this religious context Jeremiah's message seemed blasphemous – as it challenged the basis of their national and religious life. When he invited the people to 'amend their ways and their doings' so that the Lord would allow them to dwell in Jerusalem – he sounded like a prophet who had lost the plot.

> This alludes to the words of the Jerusalem liturgy that were boldly, endlessly and uncritically repeated. Jeremiah dismisses those words of the liturgy as banal and ineffective and mocks the unthinking reliance on the status quo that they reflect and embody. The accent is on trust: do not trust in, do not

count on, do not stake your life on. In one deft move the prophet has exposed the dysfunctional character of the Jerusalem temple. The temple and its royal liturgy are exposed as tools of social control which in a time of crisis will not keep their grand promises. The temple is shown not to be an embodiment of transcendence but simply an arena for social manipulation.[4]

Jeremiah declared that their worship was unacceptable to the Lord because they were neglecting to keep His commandments and laws. Ch. 7: 5-6 indicates they were worshipping other gods – idols and were unjust in their dealings with others. He exhorted them to amend their ways and not to trust in the deluded chant: 'the temple of the Lord' –as if this was a spiritual incantation that God would honour. So extreme is the situation in the Lord's eyes that he says: 'Has this house which is called by my name become a den of robbers in your eyes?'–7: 11. Brueggemann perceives that those who violated God's commandments attempted to hide in the sanctity of the temple. 'Since the text addresses the power establishment, it is fair to conclude that the crimes targeted are not simply individual acts of exploitation but are acts of the entire system.'[5]

Their neglect of God's laws brought into disrepute and invalidated the ceremonial worship. This eventually became meaningless, polluted and unacceptable to the Lord. This was so serious the severest judgment was on its way, hence the reference to the destruction of Shiloh. The peoples' failure to keep God's laws and their worship of other gods violated the integrity of the temple worship. The disastrous consequences of their idolatrous worship ultimately brought calamity and destruction to the temple. This was seen when God's people went into exile and were overwhelmed by a foe from the North predicted by Jeremiah in chapter one.

## WORSHIP THE LORD HATES

Closely aligned to worship that is unacceptable to God is worship that the Lord hates and rejects. Amos ch. 5 describes such a scene when the Lord condemns his peoples' worship in the context of his judgment on them. The Lord pulls no punches. It is as if He is going for the jugular. Simundson says: 'The Lord is about to do something so terrifying that the land will wither and dry up. The terrifying roar coming from Jerusalem is a sign that this is about to happen. The roar will send chills of fear up the spine of anyone who hears it' – 3: 4.[6] This is the roar of impending judgment.

One of the issues that surfaces in Amos as well as in Jeremiah, is that worship offered to the Lord cannot be separated from the way his people live. Jeremiah highlights that the idolatry of God's people deflected their worship from the Lord to idols – a horrendous sin to the Lord. Yet they brazenly chanted their mantra: 'the temple of the Lord' – oblivious to how abhorrent their idolatry and worship was to the Lord. Similarly in Amos ch. 5 the Lord states that his people have ignored the issues of justice and righteousness therefore their worship is counterfeit. It is neither authentic nor acceptable to the Lord. There is in fact an earlier reference to the peoples' empty worship in Amos 4: 4-5:

> Come to Bethel and transgress, come to Gilgal and multiply transgression: bring your sacrifices every morning, your tithes every three days: offer a sacrifice of thanksgiving of that which is leavened and proclaim freewill offerings, publish them: for so you love to do, O people of Israel.

Amos mocks their worship with biting sarcasm as he invites them to come to Bethel and Gilgal and transgress. Has he like Jeremiah lost the plot? Did he not realise how controversial and offensive his words were? 'Amos is not against religious practices in themselves. The sacrifices mentioned here seem to be legitimate not the direct object of his criticism...What Amos hates is the disconnection between the outward practice of religion and injustice and oppression so prevalent in the society...But know that each time you come to the sanctuary and perform your ceremonies, your sin multiplies because of your callousness, meanness and failure to perceive God's true concern that makes the gap between your religiosity and your execution of justice all the greater.'[7]

Amos 5: 21-24 reveals how unpalatable the worship of God's people had become to him. In the Lord's eyes he rejected their worship because of their lack of justice and righteousness.

> I hate I despise your feasts and take no delight in your solemn assemblies. Even though you offer me your burnt offerings and cereal offerings, I will not accept them and the peace offerings of your fatted beasts I will not look upon. Take away from me the noise of your songs: to the melody of your harps I will not listen. But let justice roll down like waters and righteousness like an ever-rolling stream.

These are stunning words spoken by the Lord. Shocking words to his people who imagined their worship was acceptable and pleasing to him. Words intent on shocking them into seeing that their worship had become counterfeit and lacking in integrity, because it was divorced from the issues of justice and righteousness. Consequently their worship was rejected because it had become repugnant to the Lord.

> The hatred of Yahweh against the worship of his people – that is the shock of this word...the first person verb in which Yahweh discloses his reaction to their worship of him, reiterate nauseated disgust and vehement rejection.[8]

Motyer says: 'There cannot be a passage in the Bible more
deliberate in expressing divine distaste than this: I hate...
I despise...take no delight...will not accept...will not look
upon...Take away from me the noise...I will not listen.'[9]
Like a musical score each phrase builds to a climax that will
stun the listeners. Unless justice and righteousness flow out
from our lives, worship that rolls off the tongue as people
roll into worship is going nowhere.

Whether our worship is traditional or contemporary the
Lord expects our lives to embrace the qualities of justice and
righteousness in our relationships with others. We cannot
divorce the way we live from the way we worship the Lord.
Similarly we cannot give our devotion and love to idols and
come and offer the Lord our diluted allegiance. Our worship
in our private lives affects our corporate, public worship.
This implies we have a responsibility not only towards
the Lord but to one another – and towards those in our
community and wider afield. This is a reminder that our
worship should not reflect a preoccupation with ourselves to
the neglect of these issues. Our worship should aim for a
healthy balance embracing our fellowship, the community
and national and international issues.

One of the difficulties of a contemporary application of
Amos' and Jeremiah's message about worship the Lord hates
and which is unacceptable to him, is that these prophets were
addressing the nation. The political, religious and social
aspects of the nation were all inter-linked. You could not
separate one from the other as they were not independent
entities. While we can apply their message to any individual
church the unspoken implication is: 'should the Church be
calling the nation to worship the Lord and drawing peoples'
attention to living justly and righteously?' The dilemma here
is that today we do not tend to think in terms of the worship
of the nation and the issues of idolatry, justice and
righteousness being connected to the life of the nation. It

may well be that many see worship as the sole concern of the church. While the issues of justice and righteousness that Amos addressed may be seen as having national or international relevance, we may still not link them to the nation and its worship. It may well be time for the Church to discover its prophetic voice and speak out about these issues to the nation.

# CHAPTER THREE

# THE PSALMS AND WORSHIP

## INTRODUCTION

In my former Church School in Marylebone Road just off Baker Street in London, for the second lesson at 10 am every Tuesday the entire school attended church. St. Marylebone Parish Church is a very beautiful church with an ornate sanctuary, a gallery and has attractive mahogany pews. Charles Wesley lived and worked in Marylebone and is buried there with a memorial stone. Lord Byron was baptised there. Admiral Lord Nelson also worshipped there and his daughter Horatia was baptised there. At the back of the church there is the Browning Chapel commemorating the marriage of Robert Browning and Elizabeth Barrett. Sir John Stainer's oratorio, 'The Crucifixion' was written for the choir of St. Marylebone in 1886 and has been performed every Friday evening at 6.30 pm ever since. I would now greatly value worshipping in such a beautiful historic church, but as an uninformed youngster these things passed me by.

During the Church Service a Psalm was always included and whichever one was chosen, as a teenager they always struck me as boring. Not a surprising response seeing I was ignorant of their meaning and use in worship. Some years later when the Lord spoke to me about learning to praise him I began to use the Psalms as a means of praise. In later years I also came to value them because they are a model of how to share our feelings with the Lord. They express a kaleidoscope of feelings about everyday life and faith in our individual and corporate relationship with the Lord. They contain feelings of depression, elation, fear, grief, joy, praise, thanksgiving and worship. One of the things that is often missing from current worship regardless of whether it is contemporary or traditional is the opportunity to express our feelings to the Lord. Thankfully feelings about our faith and our relationship with the Lord and the deepest emotions of joy and pain may be expressed through the Psalms. Mark Ashton, Vicar of the Round Church that meets at St. Andrew the Great in Cambridge says:

> If it is no longer appropriate to chant psalms, we must find other ways to incorporate them into our services. Psalms are the main biblical medium for the expression of human emotions. (Expressions of sorrow and joy, confidence and despair, anger and elation abound in the Psalter). As the psalms have disappeared from our church services, so other expressions of human emotion have welled up, some of which are much less healthy than the psalms – and almost all of which are less biblical.[1]

## HISTORICAL BACKGROUND

Psalms 1 and 2 act as an introduction to the Psalter and 150 as the conclusion. They are divided into five sections by 41, 72, 89 and 106. Two collections are attributed to David 3-41 and 51-72 and many Psalms from 106-150 are also his. The Psalms have also been divided into a number of categories: hymns, individual laments, corporate laments, penitential, thanksgiving, wisdom and Royal Psalms. They were used in the annual national festivals and especially in Temple worship.

Broyles says:'They can be simultaneously read as liturgies, literature and prophecies...The Psalms were composed not ad hoc but with careful craftsmanship and were written not for single occasions but for recurring occasions. They were not free verses but followed established patterns and conventions and were not merely read: they were performed publicly...many of the Psalms were sung with choirs at Temple festivals such as 135: 20, 'O House of Levi praise the Lord.' Psalms 15 and 24 have long been recognised

as liturgies for worshippers entering the temple...entry into
God's Temple was obviously a momentous rite of passage
for worshippers.'[2]

'The Psalms along with Isaiah are the two Old Testament
books most quoted in the New Testament. Many are relevant
to Christology and contain titles that are applied to Christ.
Behind the whole discussion of the Psalms has been an
implicit sense that for Christians they are related to Christ. In
the New Testament there are more than 93 quotations from
more than 60 of the Psalms. Among the sayings of Jesus in
the gospels there are more quotations from the Psalter than
from any other book in the Old Testament. Not only are the
Psalms referred to in the New Testament but they and
especially the Royal Psalms have been 'applied to Christ' by
Christians...Dietrich Bonhoeffer spoke for the Church when
he viewed the Psalter as the prayer book of Christ, which
means the one who prays the Psalms is Christ and it is in
Christ that Christians then pray them.'[3]

## THE PSALMS AS HYMNS
The Psalms have played an important part in the life of the
Church throughout the centuries and commentators affirm
their central place in the Church's worship. They have been
described as 'the womb of Church music' and Ambrose
considers them 'the voice of the Church.'[4] Athanasisus said:
'It is my view that in the words of this book the whole
of human life, its basic spiritual conduct and as well as its
occasional movement and thoughts, is comprehended and
contained.'[5] Bonhoeffer also wrote: 'The Psalter occupies
a unique place in the Holy Scriptures. It is God's Word
and with a few exceptions the prayer of men as well.'[6]
Westermeyer reminds us that the Psalms are used in a variety
of worship settings by different denominations. They can be
used in the Eucharist to congregational forms of morning or
evening worship, in the monastic offices and in 'free church'
worship. They also have a place in Hebrew worship.[7] The

Psalms were an integral part of the corporate worship of
Israel and her common hymn book. Weiser alludes to this
when he says: 'The Psalter has been called 'the hymn book
of the Jewish Church' and that with some justification, for it
contains the various features which point to the cultic use of
the Psalms in the worship of the Temple and especially in the
synagogue service in late Judaism.'[8]

## A MODEL OF LAMENT

The Psalms are Israel's religious poetry in the context of
her covenant relationship with God. Often they contain a
dialogue with the Lord from the perspective of the individual
or the community. Brueggeman echoes this: 'The Psalms are
helpful because they are a genuinely dialogical literature that
expresses both sides of the conversation of faith. On the one
hand as von Rad has seen Israel's faithful speech addressed
to God is the substance of the Psalms.'[9] One aspect of
this dialogue is of particular relevance to the worship of
God's people today. This is found in the Psalms that have
been identified as individual or communal lament. These are
prayers that are a cry for help, for justice, or deliverance.
Brueggemann thinks this dialogue has enormous theological
significance in the faith and liturgy of Israel and the Church.
He suggests that this dialogue of faith permits those making
petitions to be taken seriously, so that God who is addressed
is engaged in the crisis in a way that puts Him at risk. He
believes the unmitigated supremacy of God is questioned,
therefore the lament concerns a redistribution of power –
otherwise docility and submissiveness are engenderd.[10] He
astutely says:

> Where lament is absent, covenant comes into being
> only as a celebration of joy and well-being. Or in
> political categories the greater party is surrounded
> by subjects who are always 'yes-men and women'
> from whom 'never is heard a discouraging word.'
> Since such a celebrative, consenting silence does not

square with reality covenant minus lament is finally a practice of denial, cover-up and pretense, which sanctions social control...where the capacity to initiate lament is absent one is left only with praise and doxology. God is then omnipotent always to be praised. The believer is nothing and can praise or accept guilt uncritically where life with God does not function properly.[11]

Brueggemann's thesis seems to suggest that God has to be cajoled by convincing argument to act when His people need help. Here the implication is that the Lord actually has to be invited to engage in His people's struggles. It also implies His involvement is lost if He is not asked to participate. We can interpret the dialogue of faith between the Lord and His people, as one that appeals to God's faithfulness, His steadfast love and justice and His saving activity. In this context the Lord invites our faith to tenaciously appeal to Him in this dialogue. In turn this prompts Him to act on our behalf.

Brueggemann is sympathetic to those who suffer or are in pain, in the context of worship that only embraces the dimension of a celebratory style. He sympathises because the message it conveys is that everything in our lives is right and everything in the world is right. Such worship denies those who lament the opportunity to enter into dialogue with God. It prevents them from expressing their grief and loss to the Lord in the midst of the worshipping community. Pete Ward echoes a similar concern about charismatic worship: 'Charismatic worship has no reflex which may accommodate those who are grieving or in the darker corners of spiritual experience. As a result some of the songs and the worship become a problem for some charismatics. Some speak of the tone and the language of the worship songs as a cause of spiritual harm in their lives...they feel that their spiritual journey is more complex and ambiguous than what seems to be allowed in the regular worship of the church.'[12] Brueggemann voices a similar concern that identifies this as a serious issue.

> A community of faith that negates lament soon concludes that the hard issues of justice are improper questions to pose at the throne, because the throne only seems to be a place of praise...The point of access for serious change has been forfeited when the propriety of this speech is denied.[13]

A community whose genre is primarily the 'feel good factor of worship' may inadvertently be in the process of becoming self-indulgent and narcisstic. Such worship also runs the risk of preventing the Lord from engaging in a meaningful way with His people and their deepest struggles. Unwittingly, this worship borders on being idolatrous, because God has been reduced to the level of comfort praise. Westermeyer says: 'In the Psalms we deal with the height and depth of human life articulated in a most compelling way. We see our struggles against the backdrop of God's goodness – our struggles with God and God's struggles with us in steadfast love and faithfulness.'[14] The Psalms do indeed allow the individual and the Christian community to articulate and express their struggles that even traditional worship often bypasses or ignores.

The laments of Africans in diaspora America show how these Lament Psalms were used and became part of African spirituality. In 1925 two brothers Joshua and Rosamund Weldon published a collection of popular spirituals which included: 'Swing Low, Sweet Chariot,' 'Go Down Moses,' 'Roll Jordan Roll,' 'Little David,' 'Joshua Fit The Battle Of Jericho,' Play on Yo Harp' and 'Steal Away to Jesus.' All these songs except for 'Steal Away' use themes and imagery from ancient Israel and most of the biblical images used in the spirituals are from the Old Testament.[15]

R. Redman elucidates further on the use of lament songs in African spirituality: 'Because it was dangerous for slaves worshipping God they gathered in clandestine meetings held in cabins or outdoors that often lasted all night. The call to worship went out long before the meeting began as slaves passed word of the gathering to each other in the code found in such songs such as 'Steal Away to Jesus' or 'Get You Ready There's A Meeting Here Tonight.'[16]

We should take care to note that not all the Lament Psalms result in circumstantial struggles being resolved immediately which was also true for the African slaves. In this context what is important is the opportunity to express to the Lord through the dialogue of faith – our emotional, psychological and spiritual struggles and call on the Lord to be involved in them. We should also take care to note that the Lament Psalms of the individual and the community in Israel, were prayers that were paradigms of hope. Similarly the African spiritual lament songs strengthened faith and gave hope of better things to come – albeit possibly in the next world.

## WORLD-MAKING PRAISE

Sigmund Mowinckel's ground breaking study sees the Psalms as creative liturgical acts of praise. He sees praise as an act embracing an alternative future – that is it ushers in a new way God's creative action in the world. Brueggemann speaks about Mowinckel's thesis of praise and worship as being constitutive – that is the notion that they are world-making. Similarly Westermeyer says: 'God's people impose order, shape, sequence, pattern and meaning on already existing elements which are disordered and chaotic until acted upon – and in the sense that God has authorised this activity and is known to be present in it.'[17]

Mowinckel's thesis advocates that as God's people praise and worship Him in response the Lord renews their faith – and His gracious activity is released in a new way in their lives. This can be likened to the impact of prayer offered up to God, in response to which the Lord graciously acts in the lives of His people. Therefore prayer, praise and worship may be seen to release God's creative activity into our lives and is 'world-making' in the sense of ushering in something new. Brueggemann believes that 'praise is constitutive of theological reality. It not only addresses the God who is there before us, but is also an act of constructing the theological world in which we shall interact with God. Because praise is constitutive as well as responsive, practitioners of praise would do well to be critical, knowing and intentional about the enterprise of construction.'[18]

Brueggemann's and Mowinckel's understanding of the constitutive power of praise, draws our attention to being aware of the creative power of prayer, praise and worship that God's people offer up to him. This challenges us to move beyond praise and worship being only a joyful activity we offer to the Lord that makes us feel good. Brueggemann's theology asserts:

> ...the human vocation of praise is to maintain and transform the world, obtain blessing that would not be obtained, maintained or transformed, except through this routine and most serious activity authorised by God and enacted by human agents. 'World-making' is done by God...Praise is not a response to a world already fixed and settled, but is a responsive and obedient participation in a world yet to be decreed through this liturgical act.[19]

This calls for a renewed understanding of what exactly it is God's people are doing when they come to offer praise. In what ways are they contributing to God's 'world-making' in their lives, in their communities and in the world? In what ways is their praise ushering in God's kingdom?

## PSALM 22

Psalm 22 is holy ground. It speaks to us about the emotional, physical and psychological suffering of Christ on the cross. Inspired by the Holy Spirit David writes personally and without knowing it prophetically portrays the suffering of Christ. We can approach this Psalm in two ways. We can view it as a Lament Psalm – a cry and a prayer for help Christians down the centuries have made their own. Alternatively, we can view it as a prayer from Christ's lips. This Psalm also clearly divides into two sections. The first 21 verses are a prayer of lament voicing acute suffering, whereas verses 22-31 are a testimony to the Lord's deliverance. Weiser says:

> The song first leads us down into the uttermost depths of suffering, a suffering which brought the worshipper to the brink of the grave and reduced him to utter despair. It then soars to the heights of a hymn of praise and thanksgiving, sung in response to the answering of the prayer...The poet who composed the Psalm has the gift of describing his sufferings in words which deeply move our hearts and in figurative language which grips our imagination. His lamentation is one of the most touching in the Psalter.[20]

The Lament Psalms have a basic structure that enables the individual or the community to express their prayer for help to the Lord. Intense feelings that are often overpowering are expressed in the context of a covenant relationship with the Lord. These strong emotions are voiced as a dialogue of faith by focusing on God and his character and saving activity. The Lament Psalms alternate between expressing feelings and focusing on God. Towards the end of these Psalms there is usually a resolution – an answer to prayer resulting in praise and thanksgiving. This either comes in the form of the situation being resolved or how the psalmist feels being addressed, so he can rise above the situation that threatened his life and greatly troubled him.

Claus Westermann also identifies this basic structure of the Lament Psalms and sees five elements integral to them. '* Address – introductory petition: * lament: * confession of trust: * petition: * vow of praise. The address is an introductory cry for help and turning to God. The lament shares the situation with the Lord and the petition is a prayer for help. The confession of trust becomes an assurance of being heard and the vow of praise is offered when the petition has been answered.'[21]

It is reassuring to know that in Scripture the Lord shares His feelings for His people and the world. He is not a God who is detached but emotionally involved with His creation. Through the Psalms the Lord invites us, indeed gives us permission to share our feelings with Him too, because they are an integral part of our humanity made in His likeness. He doesn't expect us to hide or repress our emotions. In Psalm 22 the Lord gives us a model of how to share our feelings with Him and how to have emotional intimacy in our relationship with Him. Psalm 22 speaks about King David's fear of his enemies that play on his mind as Saul and his soldiers have been pursing him on and off for a number of years to kill him. Understandably, every now and then fear and panic grip his heart and greatly trouble his mind. As we look at this Psalm it may well remind us of our own particular issues that also trouble us.

1-2     My God, my God, why have you forsaken me? Why are you so far from helping me, from the words of my groaning? O my God I cry by day, but you do not answer: and at night but find no rest.

David shares his feelings with the Lord because he feels He has forgotten and forsaken him. God is silent and He has not answered his prayer. David is becoming desperate as God whom he knows intimately seems to have abandoned him. Emotionally and psychologically he is almost panicking and he needs some assurance from the Lord that He is going to help him.

Why is the Lord ignoring his prayer for help? Why isn't He answering him? Perhaps there is sin in his life that has not been confessed? As David doesn't mention this anywhere in the psalm we can rule this out. We can perceive that the Lord is teaching him to trust Him despite how he feels. He is drawing out his trust even though He is silent. The Lord is teaching David to view how he feels in the light of His character. And to remember the Lord's faithfulness, His steadfast love and past deliverance. He is being forced to consider that while his feelings are real they may be misleading and way off beam about the silence of God.

3-5    Yet you are holy, enthroned on the praises of Israel. In you our fathers trusted: they trusted and you delivered them. To you they cried and were saved: in you they trusted and were not disappointed.

Why does David focus on the Lord's character and how does this help him? He recalls that God is reigning, enthroned on the praises of Israel. A reminder the Lord is sovereign and in control of his life. He remembers the Lord's past faithfulness in answering His peoples' prayers when they trusted him and were not disappointed. Focusing on the Lord in this way helps him to express his feelings of abandonment and disappointment. This also begins to renew his faith and hope in the Lord as he focuses on God's faithfulness.

6-8    But I am a worm and no man: scorned by men and despised by people. All who see me mock at me, they make mouths at me, they wag their heads. He committed his cause to the Lord: let Him deliver him, let Him rescue him, for He delights in him!

David began this Psalm by sharing how he feels because the Lord is not answering his prayer and then he focused on God's character. Now he shares with the Lord how he feels because of his enemies. His self-esteem has been assaulted and he has no confidence in himself. His imagination is running wild and getting things out of perspective as he pictures what people are saying about him. He feels scorned and despised. He feels humiliated and insignificant. He feels his enemies are laughing at him and ridiculing him. They taunt him by implying that God is not going to help and rescue him. And this only adds to his agony of mind.

9-11   Yet you are the one who took me from my mother's womb: you kept me safe upon my mother's breasts. Upon you I was cast from my birth and since my mother bore me you have been my God. Be not far from me for trouble is near and there is none to help.

After sharing for a second time how he feels with the Lord David again focuses on God's character. He casts his mind back to when he was young to describe a fond tenderness in his relationship with Him. He reminds the Lord of His protection and how he relied on Him from a very young age. This is in sharp contrast to feeling abandoned by Him at the beginning of this Psalm. He reminds the Lord of the emotional intimacy that was the hallmark of his relationship with Him. But the awareness of the Lord's absence instead of His familiar presence, has left David feeling acutely vulnerable.

12-21  Many bulls encompass me, strong bulls of Basham surround me: they open wide their mouths at me like a ravening and roaring lion. I am poured out like water and all my bones are out of joint, my heart is like wax it is melted within my breast: my strength is dried up like a potsherd, and my tongue cleaves to my jaws: thou dost lay me in the jaws of death. Dogs are round about me: a company of evildoers encircle me: they have pierced my hands and feet – I can count all my bones – they stare and gloat over me: they divide my garments among them and for my raiment they cast lots. But thou O Lord be not far off! O thou my help hasten to my aid! Deliver my soul from the sword, my life from the power of the dog! Save me from the mouth of the lion, my afflicted soul from the horns of the wild oxen!

In these verses there is an atmosphere of mounting tension. David is now panicking as he imagines what his enemies might do when they capture him. A frightening scenario that emotionally and psychologically overwhelms him, as he is now beginning to feel desperate and exhausted. He can imagine being pinned to the ground and tortured by them. He visualises a terrifying scene as they gloat over him as a prisoner. His anxiety and tension mount as he now fears for his life when he says: 'Thou dost lay me in the dust of death.' This suggests that the Lord allowed this to happen to him. This was an alarming prospect when David thought about the Lord's protection in the past.

As the Lord has been silent and apparently deaf to David's request for help and as he feels abandoned by Him, he vividly describes the situation so that the Lord might be prompted into action. The prospect of what might happen to David has reached the stage where he is panicking. His prayer for help invites the Lord to: 'be not far off' – 'hasten to my aid' –'deliver my soul' – 'save me from the mouth of the lion.'

In verses 22-31 there is a transition with David rejoicing in the Lord because He has answered his prayer. It is helpful to be aware that David's enemies were his Achilles heel and his psychological weakness. This is clearly seen as in around half of his psalms (appx 37), his enemies are the subject of his prayer for help. A brief look at some of David's Psalms enables us to see the extent of his fear concerning his enemies. Psalm 31: 11-13: 'I am a reproach among all my enemies but especially among my neighbours, and am repulsive to my acquaintances: those who see me outside flee from me. I am forgotten like a dead man out of mind: I am like a broken vessel. For I hear the slander of many: fear is on every side: while they take counsel against me they scheme to take away my life.' Psalm 55: 2-6: 'I am overcome by trouble. I am distraught by the noise of the enemy because of the oppression of the wicked. For they bring trouble upon me and in anger they cherish enmity against me. My heart is in anguish against me, the terrors of death have fallen upon me. Fear and trembling come upon me and horror overwhelms me. And I say, 'O that I had wings like a dove! I would fly away and be at rest.' Psalm 69: 1-4, 'Save me O God! For the waters have come up to my neck. I sink in deep mire where there is no foothold. I have come into deep waters and the flood sweeps over me. I am weary with my crying: my throat is parched. My eyes grow dim with waiting for my God. More in number than the hairs of my head are those who hate me without cause: mighty are those who would destroy me, those who would attack me with lies.'

Verses 22-31 mark a turning point not only in Psalm 22 but also in how David feels. In hindsight he can see that the Lord is faithful and trustworthy even when he is silent. Even when He is not answering his prayer the way he anticipated and when he expected. Through this particular event in his life the Lord taught David to share his feelings with Him and to trust Him. The situation in now clearly resolved although we are not told how. This is frustrating because the sense of desperation in David's prayer was palpable. We do not know if he was getting paranoid and exaggerating how much his life was in danger from his enemies. Yet clearly something has happened between verse 21 and 22 as the Lord has answered his prayer. But we do not know if this involved rescuing him from the hands of his enemies, or merely resolving how he was feeling because of them. Now David cannot contain himself and he bursts forth into praise to testify to God's goodness in the great congregation. Weiser says:

> The darkness which filled the worshipper's soul has vanished and rejoicing with great joy he begins to sing a song of thanksgiving. He has become assured that his prayer has been answered and that God has helped him...Having been delivered by God the psalmist is so fully conscious of his happiness which has been brought about by the re-establishment of his communion with God, that even the fact that he is now able to give thanks to God is accepted by him as a gift from God's hands. As a visible sign of his gratitude he will pay a votive offering in the midst of the godly ones and invite the poor to a meal so that they may share his happiness.[22]

### PSALM 22 AND CHRIST

James Mays identifies Psalm 22 with Christ in a most insightful way. We are familiar with the connection between this Psalm and Jesus' cry on the cross: 'Eloi, Eloi, lema sabachthani' which is a direct quote of the first verse (Matt. 27:46, Mark 15:34). He points out that citing the first words of a text was in the tradition of the time a way of identifying an entire passage. The very experience of the psalmist becomes a commentary on Jesus' passion on the cross. 'In the intellectual world of Judaism one of the most important ways of understanding the meaning of present experience, was to make sense of the contemporary by perceiving and describing it in terms of an established tradition.

Because of the close connection of Psalm 22 with Jesus, the custom developed in the early church of taking the psalm as Jesus' words and relocating it completely in a Christological context. This results in understanding the

psalm in terms of Jesus. But the canonical relation between
passion narrative and psalm invites us also to understand
Jesus in terms of the psalm – that is, to view him through the
form and language of this prayer...Its language was designed
to give individuals a poetic and liturgical location to provide
a prayer that is paradigmatic for particular suffering and
needs. To use it was to set oneself in its paradigm.'[23]

Mays reminds us that the use of Psalm 22 in Holy Week
helps us to understand this psalm in the context of Jesus'
suffering. When this psalm is read on Good Friday we
immediately identify the one speaking as Jesus and gain a
glimpse into his emotional and psychological anguish – and
how acute was his sense of abandonment on the cross. 'In its
unity the psalm provides a scenario for reflection on the
significance of Jesus' death and resurrection, that is different
from the traditional models of sacrifice.

The psalm interprets Jesus' passion and resurrection as
a theodicy for those who commit their way to the Lord.
The gospel accounts make it clear that Jesus suffered and
died as one of the 'lowly.'...For the lowly, the passion and
resurrection of Jesus are a justification of God in whom they
trust and a vindication of their trust...The psalm suggests
that we think of the Lord's Supper as a thanksgiving for the
lowly. It is the Eucharist instituted and defined by a lowly
one and shared by the lowly. This raises a question about the
self-understanding we bring to the Lord's table, and whether
we come as one of the lowly.'[24]

## CHAPTER FOUR

## CHRIST AND WORSHIP

### CHRIST IS LORD

In his relationship with Christ in Philippians 3: 8 Paul speaks about 'the surpassing worth of knowing Christ Jesus my Lord.' This closeness did not suddenly occur overnight after his conversion. It is the outcome of his dedication in serving Christ and his desire to know him intimately. At the heart of Paul's ministry and spirituality is the truth that Jesus is Lord. F. W. Beare aptly remarks: 'Here and here alone in his writing, do we find the intensely personal 'Christ Jesus my Lord' – and it would be a dull reader indeed who did not mark the warm and deep devotion which breathes through every phrase...This same person Paul remarkably calls 'my Lord.' In using the singular pronoun rather than the plural 'our'– the apostle is in no way suggesting that his relationship to Christ is exclusive. Rather, the wonder of this knowledge of Christ Jesus as his Lord is so great, and the relationship so intensely personal that he focuses upon it in his testimony.'[1]

The centrality of Jesus as Lord in Paul's worship of Christ and in his theology, is seen from his letters that always have an introductory reference: to 'our Lord Jesus Christ' or 'the Lord Jesus Christ.' 'The earliest Christian writings are Paul's letters and they provide evidence for the origin of a practice of referring to Christ as 'Lord' that antedates the apostle. From his earliest letters onwards he applies 'kurios'–'Lord' to Jesus without explanation or justification, suggesting that his readers were familiar with the term and its connotation...The frequently occurring references to Jesus simply as 'the Lord'– 1Thess. 1: 6, shows how the term had acquired such a familiar usage for Christ that no further identification was necessary. Paul's letters presume a familiarity with the term as a Christological title from the earliest stages of his ministry.'[2]

In Paul's day in Aramaic, in Hebrew and in Greek, the term for master or lord was used in two ways. This could be used when addressing persons who were socially superior and also when addressing deities. Equally, there would have been political overtones associated with this title, as Caesar would have been addressed as lord. The use of lord in these ways made its application to Christ striking – and to address Christ as Lord personally or as an act of worship, may well have been interpreted as subversive and a challenge to Roman rule. M. Hooker says: 'In the Roman Empire emperors came to claim divine honours and as a result there was a growing emphasis on the imperial cult. Though Paul himself did not challenge the claims made by the state of his day – Rom. 13: 1-7, he would certainly have refused to acknowledge Caesar as kurios had that been demanded of him. By the end of the first century AD the confessions that 'Jesus is Lord' and 'Caesar is Lord' were recognised as expressing conflicting loyalties, and the proclamation of Christ was seen as subversive.'[3]

Paul would have known that the use of the term Lord had a religious association in the life and worship of Israel. The Jews did not actually pronounce the name of God –Yahweh but instead used other forms by which to address him. In Hebrew God was often referred to as 'adonay'– 'the Lord.' In the first century this could be used as a substitute for the name of God and addressing Christ as 'Lord' conferred on him the status of and worship as God. Anyone who was familiar with the O. T. would not fail to recognise the allusion of 'Lord' to Isaiah 45: 22-23: 'And there is no other god besides me, a righteous God and Saviour: there is no one beside me. Turn to me and be saved all the ends of the earth! For I am God and there is no other. By myself I have sworn, from my mouth has gone forth in righteousness a word that

shall not return: To me every knee shall bow and every
tongue swear allegiance.' Dunn says:

> What is astonishing, however, is that these words in
> Isaiah are spoken by God and in one of the most
> unyielding monotheistic passages in the whole Bible.
> At the very least we have to recognise that the
> Philippian hymn – 2: 6-11, envisaged acclamation of
> and reverence before Christ, which, according to
> Isaiah, God claimed for himself alone. On any count
> that is an astonishing transfer for any Jew to make.

Even as Lord Jesus acknowledges his Father as God. Here
it becomes plain that 'kurios' is not so much a way of
identifying Jesus with God, but if anything more a way of
distinguishing Jesus from God. We may note also from 1 Cor.
3: 23, 'you are Christ's and Christ is God's' and in 11: 3 'the
head of Christ is God.' And again in 1 Cor. 15: 24-28, 'the
Lord of all.' Christ has been given his lordship by God and it
is a lordship that will in the end be wholly subject to God.

The only obvious resolution of the tension set up by
Paul's talk of Jesus as Lord, then, is to follow the logic
suggested by his reference of Yahweh texts to Jesus as Lord
(as above). That is, that Jesus' lordship is a status granted by
God, a sharing in his authority. It is not that God has stepped
aside and Jesus has taken over. It is rather that God shared
his Lordship with Christ without it ceasing to be God's
alone.'[4] But it is more than that. It is a sharing of worship
that is also conferred on Christ as God.

In Paul's letter to the Philippians in 2: 6-11, Christ is
exalted as Lord by his Father because of his obedience and
this is commonly known as the 'Philippian Hymn.'

> Christ Jesus who, though he was in the form of God,
> did not count equality with God a thing to be grasped,
> but emptied himself, taking the form of a servant,
> being born in the likeness of men. And being found
> in human form he humbled himself and became
> obedient unto death, even death on a cross.
> Therefore, God has highly exalted him and bestowed
> on him the name which is above every name, that at
> the name of Jesus every knee should bow, in heaven
> and on earth and under the earth, and every tongue
> confess that Jesus Christ is Lord, to the glory of God
> the Father.

Concerning Christ's exaltation as Lord, O'Brien sees 'God
the Father as decisively intervening and acting on Jesus'
behalf. Jesus' self-humbling reached the absolute depths in
his most shameful death, a death on a cross. But now, by
way of vindication and approval of Jesus' total self-
humbling, the Father has magnificently exalted his Son to
the highest station and graciously bestowed upon him the
name above all other names, this is, his own name, Lord
(Yahweh), along with all that gives meaning and substance
to the name. In his exalted state Jesus now exercises
universal lordship...It is not implied that Jesus' eventual
exaltation was the incentive for his temporary humiliation:
otherwise the humbling would have been no true humiliation
at all, and as such would have been self-regarding, not self-
denying.'[5]

There is also a liturgical as well as an eschatological
nuance implied in the exaltation of Jesus as Lord. In 1
Corinthians the references to Jesus as Lord indicate that this
title was an integral aspect of their worship – for instance in
10: 21 & 11: 17-38. Also in 16: 22 we have 'Maranatha' –
'Come Lord Jesus.' For Christians in Paul's day the
emphasis on every 'knee shall bow' expressed submission in
worship to Jesus – worship that previously had been directed

only to God. But now God has conferred on Jesus divine status that qualifies him to be the recipient of worship too. In the early church there was a political cutting-edge to the acclamation 'Jesus is Lord' and 'bowing the knee to Jesus' – as this was seen as subversive to the homage Caesar demanded. Similarly Fee says: 'We should note finally that this declaration of Jesus as 'Lord,' would probably not be lost on believers in a city whose inhabitants are Roman citizens and who are devotees of 'lords many,' including 'lord Caesar.' Paul well knows to whom he is writing these words, especially since he is one of the emperor's prisoners and the Philippians are suffering at the hands of Roman citizens as well.'[6]

As well as having contemporary relevance in Paul's day 'Jesus is Lord' also has perennial significance, as Christians down the centuries have offered worship to their Lord. Equally, there is an eschatological dimension to the acclamation 'Jesus is Lord,' because at the *'parousia'* – the second coming every knee shall bow in worship at Jesus' feet. Because God has given Jesus the name that is above every name he exercises authority and power on a universal scale. Therefore, Jesus' Lordship has a cosmic and an eternal dimension to it. 'There is in this language no hint that those who bow are acknowledging his salvation: on the contrary they will bow to his sovereignty at the end, even if they are not yielding to it now.'[7]

Concerning the universal Lordship conferred on Jesus by God O'Brien says: 'This bestowal by God is the rarest of all honours, in view of his assertion in Isaiah 42: 8: 'I am the Lord, that is my name: my glory I give to no other.'...God not only gave Jesus a designation which distinguished him from all other beings, a title which outranked all other titles. He also conferred on him all that coincided with that title, giving substance and meaning to it. In his exalted state Jesus has a new rank involving the exercise of universal lordship...All authority in heaven and on earth were his by nature as well as by gift.'[8] And as we have already noted Jesus' lordship has also bestowed upon him the honour of receiving worship that previously was only directed towards God.

## CHRIST A HIGH PRIEST

Within Evangelical spirituality the Lordship of Christ is a theme Christians are familiar with. Yet in comparison the relevance of Christ as a high priest in our faith and worship is neglected. While we speak about Christ as our friend, our Saviour and Lord, we do not expound the relevance and richness of Christ as our high priest. Yet the book of Hebrews eloquently bears witness to Christ's priesthood. D. Peterson the Principal of Oak Hill says about Hebrews: 'This is truly essential reading for those who would establish a theology of Christian worship. The writer takes up a number of Old Testament themes and shows how they remain an essential foundation for our thinking...A God ordained priesthood, authentic sacrifices, and effective cleansing and sanctification must be provided for those who would draw near to God and serve him.

The writer also shows us, however, how these foundational Old Testament themes must be re-interpreted in the light of their fulfillment in Christ. Indeed, our understanding of the person and work of Christ can be greatly enriched by viewing the central truths of the gospel in terms of transformed worship categories. The perfect sacrifice of Jesus provides the basis of relating to God under the new covenant. His high-priestly work secures a once-for all atonement for sin, the cleansing of our consciences and continuing right access to God. Expressed in other terms, this means participation by faith now in the joyful assembly of all God's people in the heavenly Jerusalem. This certainty of access to God in the present is the guarantee of literal participation in the coming kingdom or city of God.'[9]

## CHRIST A MERCIFUL PRIEST

'Therefore, Christ had to be made like his brethren in every respect, so that he might become a merciful and faithful high priest in the service of God, to make atonement for the sins of the people. For, because he himself has suffered and been tempted, he is able to help those who are tempted' – Heb. 2: 17-18. One aspect of being a priest is to represent the people to God and God to His people. As a result the priest identifies with the people he represents and indeed has a solidarity with them. Heb. 2: 17-18 clearly indicates that the same is true of Christ. F. F. Bruce says: 'Any priest must be one with those whom he represents before God and this is equally so with Christ as his peoples' high priest. In order to serve them in this capacity he was obliged to become completely like his brothers and sisters – apart from sin, of course...He is merciful because through his own sufferings and trials he can sympathise with theirs: he is faithful because he endured to the end without faltering,'[10] Mercy is an attribute of God that is mentioned in Ex. 34: 19 when Moses made a request to see God's glory. Here the merciful nature of Christ reflects the mercy of God that is intrinsic to his character. God may execute his judgment but he is also inclined to be merciful to those who are penitent too. And that mercy has been clearly shown by Christ on the cross.

Despite our sin Christ is a merciful high priest, not one who stands over us in judgment and who condemns us. As Isa. 1: 18 reminds us – 'Come now let us reason together says the Lord: 'Though your sins are like scarlet they shall be white as snow: though they are red like crimson they shall become like wool.' Christ is our merciful Lord who can cleanse us from our sin and take away our guilt.

## CHRIST A COMPLETE PRIEST

Hebrews is resplendent with priestly and sacrificial images about Christ and portrays him as a high priest who has passed into the heavens – Heb. 4:14. He is a minister in the sanctuary and true tent which is set up not by man but by the Lord – Heb. 8: 1-2. As we recall God's initiative in giving Moses detailed instructions about building the tabernacle and the ark, setting up the sacrificial system and appointing priests – here we are also reminded that Christ being appointed a high priest in the heavenly sanctuary, is also God's initiative too.

'Priesthood and sacrifice are inseparable entities'[11] and in this symbolic book of scripture about Christ the author compares priesthood and the sacrificial system in the Old Testament, with Christ our high priest and what he has achieved through his sacrificial death on the cross. The writer expounds some wonderful truths about Christ's complete priesthood – (complete in the sense that it is perfect and lacks nothing) which supersedes anything the priests in the Old Testament accomplished. F. F. Bruce says:

> The author was not a complete innovator in presenting Christ as his peoples' high priest, but he elaborates the priesthood of Christ in quite a distinctive manner, and he does so in order to establish that in Christ and the gospel God has spoken his final and perfect word to mankind.[12]

Raymond Brown succinctly highlights certain aspects of Christ's complete priesthood. He see this as victorious because Christ's sacrifice for sin is complete and does not have to be repeated – whereas in the Old Testament sacrifices had to be constantly repeated. He also sees three strands of truths connected to Christ's priesthood. Firstly, Christ as a high priest surpasses the Old Testament priests because he has made their sacrifices obsolete. Secondly, Christ is also portrayed as a human priest. One who knows, understands and who sympathises with our weaknesses, although he himself is perfect – Heb. 4: 15. Thirdly, Christ is a unique priest because he is the Son of God as united with his divinity is his humanity.[13] There is also a fourth aspect of Christ's priesthood which Brown does not mention from this context in Heb. 4: 14-16. Namely, that Christ's sacrifice as a priest was possible because he was sinless 4: 15. A reminder of the purity of sacrifice without blemish offered in the Old Testament.

## CHRIST A COMPASSIONATE PRIEST

Hebrews mentions the compassionate priesthood of Christ. 'For we have not a high priest who is unable to sympathise with our weaknesses, but one who in every respect has been tempted as we are, yet without sinning' – Heb. 4: 15. In our struggle with temptation and besetting sin, what is reassuring is the awareness that Jesus himself experienced his own particular temptations and testings. A. T. H. Robinson says: 'His whole life was one of temptation and the very fact that he had powers and abilities which we do not have only added to the stress.'[14] Although we only have a record of Jesus being tempted by the devil in the wilderness, we can readily imagine that these insidious temptations came Jesus' way more often. P. Ellingworth perceives that Christ's earthly life gives him inner understanding of human experience and thus makes him ready and able to give active help.[15] C. R. Kroester sees that sympathy is a heartfelt bond that is expressed in acts of mercy towards those who suffer and reflects the cultural context of Jesus' day:

> Jesus the high priest is identified by his ability to sympathise with the weak. Speakers in antiquity understood that listeners were moved not only by logic but also by appeals to emotion and character. Therefore before engaging in exegetical argument, the author seeks to touch the feelings of the listeners inviting them to identify with the high priest who has identified with them. Christ manifests sympathy because he has been tested as the listeners have (Heb 4: 15). They had previously been denounced,

abused, dispossessed and imprisoned (10: 32-34): and continued to experience friction with others in society (13: 13). Some remained in prison (13: 3). Those familiar with traditions concerning Jesus' passion would know that he too was denounced, abused and imprisoned.[16]

Heb. 4: 15 – 5: 4 also reminds us that priests in the Old Testament had three qualifications. Firstly, they were called by God to act on behalf of men. Secondly, a priest had to be sympathetic so he could deal gently with the ignorant and wayward since he himself is beset with weakness. Thirdly, a priest being aware of his own sinfulness also had to offer sacrifices for his own sins. We know that Christ was called by God to be a priest and that he is sympathetic and compassionate because he identifies with our temptations, as he himself was tempted throughout his earthly life. Because of Jesus' total identification with us and his compassion towards us in our struggles – Heb. 4:16 we are reminded: 'We may come with confidence to the throne of grace, that we may receive mercy and help in time of need, because of Christ our great high priest.' We are assured of Jesus' understanding and sympathy in the midst of our struggles, temptations and weaknesses: and he exhorts us not to be discouraged or to despair. His invites us to come and ask for his help whatever our circumstances may be.

## CHRIST A SUBMISSIVE PRIEST
Heb. 5: 4-8 speaks about Christ's submissive priesthood. He did not presume to reach out for, grasp, or exalt himself to the status of a high priest. Christ was called and appointed by God because of his obedience, his godly reverence and his sinlessness. His priesthood was rooted in his submission as God's servant during his earthly life. We read in Heb. 5: 8: 'Although he was a Son, he learned obedience through what he suffered.' The submission of Christ to the Father is a

sublimely selfless quality. It is a reflection of his love for God and a sign of his willingness to serve Him as a servant.

In Heb. 5: 7 there is a reference to Christ's suffering in Gethsemane when he offered up prayers with loud cries and tears. Brown reminds us of the 'spiritually daunting and humanly terrifying moment when Jesus did not resist the sovereign purposes of God. Gethsemane is the most moving example of that 'humble submission' that characterised his whole life. Even in his deepest agony he continued and maintained that same attitude of submission.'[17]

Concerning Jesus' submission F. F. Bruce says: 'He set out from the start on the path of obedience to God, and learned by the Sufferings which came his way in consequence just what obedience to God involved in practice in the conditions of human life on earth. Perhaps the obedient Servant of the Lord in Isaiah 50: 4-9 was in our author's mind. The Servant's eagerness to pay heed to the voice of God exposes him to ridicule and ill-treatment, but he accepts this as something inseparable from his obedience...So these Sufferings which Jesus endured were the necessary price of his obedience, more than that they were part and parcel of his obedience – the very means by which he fulfilled the will of God.'[18]

Koester informs us that the idea people learned by suffering was commonplace and Jesus' suffering even though he was a son – shapes the way the author's listeners see their own situation. 'They are among the sons and daughters that God is bringing to glory – 2: 10 and like Jesus the Son they are being tested. Although Jesus was never disobedient to God, he could not demonstrate obedience until he was placed in a situation where the will of God was challenged and obedience required. There was constancy in Jesus' unfailing obedience to God's will, yet as he encountered new situations, his faithfulness to God was challenged and his obedience shaped accordingly.'[19]

## CHRIST A PERMANENT PRIEST

The readers of Hebrews were Jewish Christians who were in danger of reverting to the Old Testament ceremonial rituals associated with Judaism, which explains the careful exposition of priesthood in the Old Testament in comparison to Christ's priesthood. The author has to be specific in referring to the priestly sacrificial system in order to show that Christ's sacrifice has put an end to this. He exhorts these Jewish Christians who are on the point of forsaking their commitment to Christ, to more fully hold onto their faith in him – by grasping how much more comprehensive, permanent and superlative Christ's priesthood is.

In Heb. 7 the author focuses on Christ's priesthood where he is compared to a priest after the order of Melchizedek: 'But Christ holds his priesthood permanently because he continues for ever' – 7: 24. That Christ is a priest for ever is also alluded to in 6: 19-20: 'We have this as a sure and steadfast anchor of the soul, a hope that enters into the inner shrine behind the curtain, where Jesus has gone as a forerunner on our behalf, having become high priest for ever after the order of Melchizedek.' This obscure reference to Melchizedek forms an integral part of the author's presentation about Christ. He points out that he was a priest after the order of Melchizedek that contrasted sharply with the Jewish priesthood that was after the order of Aaron. A reminder the Scriptures spoke of not one but two types of priesthood. The Levitical priesthood established by the Law and that which was after the type of Melchizedek in Psalm 110: 4. Melchizedek's priesthood was understood to be eternal and effective whereas Aaron's was temporary, imperfect and was now set aside by Christ – because of its weakness and because it was obsolete. Consequently, Jesus

is not a priest after the order of Aaron but after the order of
Melchizedek – therefore Christ's priesthood is permanent.

## CHRIST A SUPERIOR PRIEST

The author of Hebrews also emphasises the superiority of
Christ's priesthood because he exercises a far more excellent
ministry than any Jewish priest as he mediates a far better
covenant. This covenant is far superior to the old since it is
enacted – established on far better promises. Jesus our high
priest now reigning as Lord in the heavenly sanctuary
guarantees to uphold this new covenant – Heb. 7: 22. This
theme is taken up in Heb. 8: 6-13 that brings about a new
covenant relationship with God – so Christ has fulfilled the
prophetic utterance of Jeremiah 31: 34, that is alluded to in
Heb. 8: 6-7. F. F. Bruce points out that the superiority of the
covenant is because Jesus himself is the Mediator and
the better promises on which it is established will appear in
the quotation from Jer. 31: 31-34.[20]

Christ's priesthood is also far superior to that of the Jewish
priests: 'For it was fitting that we should have such a high
priest, holy, blameless, unstained, separated from sinners,
exalted above the heavens' – Heb. 7: 26. This superiority is
also emphasized in Heb. 7: 27-28: 'Christ has no need like
those high priests, to offer sacrifices daily, first for his own
sins and then for those of the people. He did this once for
all when he offered up himself.' But R. Brown also sees the
importance of the old covenant: 'Although the old covenant
is a vanishing shadow, our writer does not dismiss it hastily,
casually or unappreciatively. He recognises something of its
former glory, even when he is explaining its partial worth.'
He quotes Westcott who observes this about the author of
Hebrews: 'He seems to linger over the sacred treasures of the
past, there was he says something majestic and attractive
about the Mosaic ordinances of worship. Christians do not
doubt that, rather when they acknowledge the beauty and
meaning of the law, they understand the gospel better.'[21]

The revolutionary theology about Christ as a high priest stands in sharp contrast to the sacrifices Jewish priests formerly made. These sacrifices culminated in the high priest entering the Holy of Holies once a year on the Day of Atonement. Heb. 9: 8 reminds us: 'By this the Holy Spirit indicates that the way into the sanctuary is not yet opened as long as the outer tent is still standing.' This was a perpetual reminder that access into the very presence of God, into the Holy of Holies was restricted. Christ's sacrifice is revolutionary because he entered the heavenly sanctuary not with the blood of goats and calves – but with his own blood. And God accepted this as the final and complete offering for sin.

Therefore, the remarkable truth is that access into the very presence of God is now freely available to His people. In the Old Testament only the high priest could come into the presence of God on behalf of the people once a year on the Day of Atonement. Now those who trust in Christ have priestly access into the very presence of God. Unlimited access into the heavenly sanctuary, into the very presence of God to worship him, has been made possible by Jesus our great high priest: and drawing near to God and being in his presence, enjoying fellowship and communion with him is indeed a priestly privilege. It is much more superior to anything God's people had access to in the Old Testament.

## CHRIST AN ETERNAL PRIEST

Christ is an eternal priest because of the value God places on his blood and because of what Christ offers to God as high priest. Watchman Nee emphasises this profound truth when he points out the shed blood of Christ is effective because of the value God places on it – and because He accepted Christ's blood for the atonement of our sins.[22] R. C. Moberly says something similar when he speaks of the culminating point of sacrifice in the Old Testament.

This was not in the shedding of the blood. But in the presentation before God in the holy place, of the blood that had been shed.[23]

Therefore, Christ's ministry as a high priest in the heavenly sanctuary prepared by God is also as Moberly points out: 'Christ's eternal presentation of a life, which eternally is the life that died. And in the life which Christ eternally presents to God, Calvary is eternally implied.'[24]

Ian Bradley highlights the same truth when he says: 'Our Eucharist is the true representation of Christ's true and continuous sacrifice once for all time offered on the earth – Golgotha and perpetually presented to the Father on our behalf in Eternity.' 'It is the eternal, sacrificial activity of the resurrected and ascended Christ and through him of God, with which the Eucharist links his body on earth.'[25] Charles Wesley's eucharistic hymn replete with sacrificial imagery makes this point:

> Thou lamb that sufferest on the tree
> And in that dreadful mystery
> Still offerest up thyself to God.
> We cast us on thy sacrifice
> Wrapped in the sacred smoke arise
> And covered with atoning blood.[26]

## CHRIST A COSMIC PRIEST

As we read the book of Hebrews we glimpse the cosmic significance of Christ's priesthood: 'But when Christ had offered for all time a single sacrifice for sins, he sat down at the right hand of God' – Heb. 10: 12. Christ who is seated in heaven at the right hand of God exercises a cosmic priesthood, because his ministry extends to the heavenly places as well as to the earth. His ministry as our great high priest also transcends time and history. The cosmic impact of Christ's priesthood is also echoed in Eph. 1: 9-10: 'For God has made known to us in all wisdom the mystery of his will, according to his purpose which he set forth in Christ as a plan for the fullness of time, to unite all things in heaven and things on earth.' Col. 1: 19-20 echoes a similar truth: 'For in Christ God was pleased to reconcile to himself all things, whether on earth or in heaven, making peace by the blood of Christ's cross.' Christ's cosmic priestly ministry embraces the ministry of reconciliation and unity.

Through the gift of priestly access into the presence of God in the heavenly sanctuary, the writer of Hebrews reminds God's people of their calling as a holy nation and royal priesthood: 'Through Christ let us continually offer up a sacrifice of praise to God, that is the fruit of lips that acknowledge his name'– Heb. 13:15. Our priestly privilege in entering God's presence is not only to intercede, but also to offer up worship that overflows with thanksgiving and praise – for all that Christ our great high priest has accomplished for us. Such worship finds expression in Rev: 15: 3-4.

> And they sing a new song saying: worthy art thou to take the scroll and to open its seals for thou was slain and by your blood didst ransom men for God, from every tribe and tongue and people and nation: and hast made them a kingdom and priests to our God and they shall reign on earth.

### CHRIST A JOYFUL PRIEST

In Heb. 12: 2 we read: 'Jesus the pioneer and perfecter of our faith who for the joy that was set before him endured the cross, despising the shame and is seated at the right hand of the throne of God.' We may glimpse aspects of Jesus' priesthood that were a source of joy to him in the gospels. Although there is scant reference to Jesus' reactions to the healings and miracles he performed and about the individuals he met, we can imagine how much joy these occasions brought to him. Jesus would have experienced joy at seeing the kingdom of God having an impact in peoples' lives. He would have been joyful when people responded to him and to his teaching about God as Father. We can also readily imagine the crowds being ecstatic with joy at the healings and miracles he performed and individuals reacting in the same way when they were healed or set free by a personal encounter with Christ.

Jesus' joy is also reflected in John 15: 11 when he said to his disciples: 'These things I have spoken to you, that my joy may be in you and that your joy may be full.' F. F. Bruce says: 'It is not difficult to trace an affinity between the joy of which our author speaks here and the joy to which Jesus himself makes repeated reference in the upper room discourses of the Fourth Gospel. He tells his disciples there of his desire that his joy may be in them, so that their joy may be full (John 15: 11: cf. 16: 20-24): and in his high priestly prayer he asks the Father 'that they may have my joy fulfilled in themselves.' So here the 'joy set before him' is not something for himself alone, but something to be shared with those for whom he died as sacrifice and lives as high priest.'[27]

As Jesus discerned he was the 'suffering servant' prophesied in Isaiah, Heb. 12:2 allows us a glimpse into the joy he anticipated would result from his sacrificial death. We may perceive that his joy embraced many things, such as the joy of our salvation: the joy of seeing humanity reconciled to God: the joy of death being defeated: the joy of the coming of the Holy Spirit: the joy of anticipating his resurrection: the joy of returning to the bosom of the Father and the joy of the second coming.

## WORSHIP AS A ROYAL PRIESTHOOD
To grasp the various nuances of meaning about Christ as a high priest reinforces the truth that it is through Christ we come to offer our worship to God as 'a royal priesthood.' Christopher Gray, a priest tragically murdered in Liverpool

in 1996 refers to 1 Pet. 2: 5-9, where the people of God are described as a 'holy priesthood' and a 'royal priesthood.' He comments on these two texts: 'They suggest that the whole Christian body is called to be priestly, a royal priesthood dependent on Christ.'[28] And 'any other sort of Christian priesthood if it is to be faithful to the New Testament, must fit in with the N. T. picture of Christ as the only true priest in the full sense of the term and the whole Christian body being priestly in a secondary sense, dependent on Christ. It must be a particular ministry that is derived from Christ and promotes the priesthood of the whole body.'[29]

C. Cocksworth also alludes to the priestly people of God in Pet. 2: 9. He points out that this makes some of the strongest statements about the priestly identity of the whole people of God to be found in the New Testament – 'you are a chosen race, a royal priesthood, a holy nation, God's own people, in order that you may proclaim the mighty acts of him who called you out of darkness into his marvellous light.' This is a quote from the O. T. as God's people have always been a 'royal priesthood' – Ex. 19: 6.[30] The concept of God's people as priests who offer up worship to Him through Christ is also found in Rev. 5: 10: 'And thou has made them a kingdom and priests to our God.'

Michael Ramsey former Archbishop of Canterbury points out that Christ's priesthood is unique and unrepeatable: 'but if we shrink from saying that Christians are also to share in it, we seem compelled to say that Christians are called to reflect it. If indeed Christians are 'partakers of Christ as this Epistle says, and if they are 'carrying about in the body the dying of Jesus' as St. Paul says, then his priesthood and sacrifice, unique as they are, are to be reflected in the Christians…and Hebrews tells of priesthood and sacrifice as describing the life of the church itself.'[31]

## SPIRITUAL SACRIFICES IN WORSHIP

One aspect of the life of the church as a royal priesthood is to be expressed in our corporate worship and this is reflected in 1 Peter 2: 4-5:

> Come to Christ to that living stone rejected by men but in God's sight precious – and like living stones be yourselves built into a spiritual house, to be a holy priesthood, to offer spiritual sacrifices acceptable to God through Jesus Christ.

Peter uses a metaphor in these verses that emphasises God's people being likened to a spiritual house. Commentators see this as a direct inference to being built into a spiritual temple. P. Davids says: 'The picture of the church as a temple is not only common in the N. T. but was also known in Judaism especially in the Dead Sea Community...The concept of the non-physical church replacing the material temple in Jerusalem is widespread in Christian writings.'[32] Schreiner indicates this house is spiritual – 'because it is animated and indwelt by the Holy Spirit. Despite the hesitation of some scholars here Peter clearly identified the church as God's new temple. The physical temple pointed toward and anticipated God's new temple, and now that the new temple has arrived the old is superfluous...The purpose of such a building is that they function as a holy priesthood.'[33] And integral to priesthood is offering up spiritual sacrifices in worship to God through Christ our high priest.

Having been designated by God to be a holy and royal priesthood, reinforces that we are righteous and sanctified by Christian. Holy has the connotation of being set apart and speaks to us about consecration and dedication to God as worshippers. Schreiner says, 'The notion of the church as a priesthood anticipated verse 9. Peter was not thinking mainly of each individual functioning as a priest before God. The emphasis here is on the church corporately as God's set-apart priesthood, in which the emphasis is likely on the believers functioning as priests.'[34]

At this point it instructive to be aware as God designates his people a holy and royal priesthood, this is a title that signifies beauty and dignity. Holy is a spiritual attribute and is associated with worshipping the Lord in the context of his holiness – while royal indicates a title of dignity. Priesthood is also honour bestowed upon God's people of the highest rank in order to minister to the Lord. This is one of the most ambitious designs for His people. It also signifies great privilege in being able to come into God's presence to worship Him through Christ our high priest.

Therefore God's people offer spiritual sacrifices acceptable to the Lord. In 1 Peter 2: 9 this is seen as – declaring the wonderful deeds of him who called us out of darkness into his marvellous light. Our corporate worship is made in the context of offering spiritual sacrifices to God and we do so through the Lord Jesus Christ, our high priest: the Head of the Church and the cornerstone of the spiritual temple. So in our worship we offer sacrifices of praise and thanksgiving for our salvation: sacrifices of prayer and testimony to God's goodness: sacrifices of time and tithes: sacrifices of obedience and trust. At the same time we know from Romans 12: 1, we are able to offer by the mercies of God our bodies as a living sacrifice, holy and acceptable to God which is our spiritual worship. Being God's holy and royal priesthood has corporate implications as well as individual responsibility. It is God's desire for his people that as a holy and royal priesthood we live out the splendour of the call to worship Him.

## CHAPTER FIVE

## WORSHIP AT THE THRONE OF GOD

### ISAIAH'S VISION OF WORSHIP

One of the most remarkable things that Scripture provides us with is a glimpse into the worship that takes place in heaven. Isaiah, Ezekiel, and John on the Isle of Patmos, all had visions of worship around the throne of God. To closely look at these visions of heavenly worship can shape our worship here on earth. It is particularly interesting to note that Matt Redman a leading contemporary figure in Christian worship, recently focused in 2004 on the theme of worship at the heavenly throne. 'On several different occasions the Bible allows us a glimpse into an open heaven. Each time is a window of revelation through which we discover more of what worship look like before the heavenly throne.'

> So many clues as to what our congregational gatherings should look like are found in these accounts of the heavenly throne. When it comes to worship the throne always sets the tone. Each time we gather together we don't just journey to a church building – we journey before the very throne of God. To lose sight of this is to lose sight of the majestic in worship. Every kingdom has a king and every king a throne. And the kingdom of God is no exception. The Lord is the King above all kings and he has the throne above all thrones. There is no higher seat of authority, power and splendour in the whole of the universe. The elders bow low there, the angels encircle it and the whole host of heaven arrange themselves around it (1 Kings 22: 19). One day a countless multitude from every nation, tribe, people and tongue will gather there (Rev. 7: 9).[1]

The first 5 chapters of Isaiah speak about God's judgment on His people because of their sin. The death of Uzziah marked the end of an age of stability and the beginning of the threat by Assyria. But Isaiah ch. 6 takes us beyond human history and presents us with God's perspective on it. In ch. 6 the prophet unexpectedly has a vision of the Lord on His throne in the context of heavenly worship:

> In the year that king Uzziah died I saw the Lord sitting upon a throne, high and lifted up: and his train filled the temple. Above him stood the seraphim: each had six wings: with two he covered his face, and with two he covered his feet and with two he flew. And one called to another and said:
>
> > 'Holy, holy, holy is the Lord of hosts:
> > the whole earth is full of his glory.'
>
> And the foundations of the thresholds shook at the voice of him who called and the house was filled with smoke. And I said: 'Woe is me! For I am lost: for I am a man of unclean lips and I dwell in the midst of a people of unclean lips: for my eyes have seen the Lord of hosts!'
>
> Then flew one of the seraphim to me, having in his hand a burning coal which he had taken with tongs from the altar. And he touched my mouth and said: 'Behold this has touched your lips: your guilt is taken away and your sin is forgiven.' And I heard the voice of the Lord saying: 'Whom shall I send and who will go for us?' Then I said 'here I am! Send me.' And he said: 'Go and say to this people: 'hear and hear, but do not understand: see and see but do not perceive.'
> Isa. 6: 1-9

Although the holiness of God is a familiar concept I am not aware that sufficient attention is drawn to this in our worship.

Yet it is clear that the holiness of God is central In Isaiah's vision of heavenly worship. Such was the powerful impact of God's holiness that he became acutely aware of his sin and the sin of the nation. 'He has been made aware of the awesome holiness of God with all that means of His transcendence and yet His immanence and now he is suddenly and brutally aware of himself.'[2] Brevard Childs also reminds us – 'Holiness in the Old Testament is not an ethical quality, but the essence of God's nature as separate and utterly removed from the profane. Holiness, 'the glory of his majesty' strikes terror in the unholy and proud, (Isa. 2: 19) but to his attendants awe and reverence.'[3] The holiness of God revealed in this vision can inform and shape our worship. It can influence our approach to worship, our corporate confession, the atmosphere of our worship and our everyday lives.

Anyone having a vision of heavenly worship today would probably be ecstatic – although if it followed the pattern of Isaiah's it would not be only for their benefit. As we shall see, glimpses of heavenly worship not only have an unforgettable and life changing impact, they also contain an intrinsic call to serve the Lord. In ch. 6: 10-13 Isaiah is called to announce a message of judgment on God's people that spells out certain disaster for them – although it also contains a seed of hope and renewal. The Lord may have given him this vision of heavenly worship to reassure him about the difficult nature of his message. Oswalt says: 'The vision was clearly fundamental to the entire course of Isaiah's ministry and to the shape of his book. The glory, the majesty, the holiness and the righteousness of God became the ruling concepts of his ministry.'[4]

Isaiah may well have been taking part in the daily routine of worship when the Lord unexpectedly revealed himself and the vision of worship in the throne room of heaven. Whether or not he was actually in the temple is irrelevant although this is the context of his vision. His perception of reality and who God is has been completely shattered. He had the privilege of seeing God in all his authority and glory and holiness and majesty. This is an awe-inspiring scene as he is overwhelmed by the vision of the holiness of God in this scene of heavenly worship. He has seen the Lord exalted and high and lifted up sitting on a throne in His kingly rule. 'Isaiah feels the raw edge of terror at being where humanity dare not go.'[5] And he is almost certain to have been lying prostrate at the revelation of God's unprecedented holiness and majesty.

Isaiah saw the heavenly seraphim, servants of God around the throne who were praising Him 'in rapt attentiveness, utterly devoted to Yahweh, fluttering around the Holy One... The primary activity that fills the throne room with glad surrender is the seemingly unending doxology of the divine choir. It sings of the holiness, the splendour, the glory, the unutterable majesty of the ruler of heaven whose awesome governance extends over all the earth (the same threefold 'holy' is echoed in Rev. 4:8).'[6] The overwhelming sense of God's holiness evokes in Isaiah a sense of his inadequacy and a fresh awareness of his sinfulness and he is reduced to nothing. Oswalt also says: 'The statement that the seraphim were calling to each other is probably an indication that the singing was antiphonal – but it also may be a way of saying that they were delighting with one another in the glory of God...It can hardly be doubted that this experience accounts for the common title for God in Isaiah 'the Holy One of Israel/Jacob.'[7]

As soon as Isaiah confesses his sin and identifies with the sin of the nation the Lord takes the initiative to cleanse him. He sends one of the seraphim with a burning coal from the altar who touches his mouth as a sign that his guilt was taken away. Although he records his vision Isaiah is not the object of it. How he feels is also not the main focus although we can easily see it that way. Brueggeman in his inimitable style discerns that the Lord's forgiveness allows Isaiah a legitimate place in the very presence of God – but it is not for his enjoyment of the divine presence. 'The throne room of God is the policy room of world government. There are messages to be sent. The government of Yahweh needs a carrier.'[8] Oswalt echoes this: 'But for whatever reason, God makes it plain that while spiritual experience is never merely a means to an end, neither is it an end in itself. Unless that experience issues in some form of lived-out praise to God it will turn on itself and putrefy. That Isaiah is neither directly addressed nor coerced is suggestive. Perhaps it is so because Isaiah does not need coercion, but further needs an opportunity to respond.'[9] Similarly Childs perceives:

> Indeed the focus throughout is not on the spiritual experience of the prophet or on what this ecstatic event meant to him. To focus on such an individual, personal evaluation completely misses the point of the narrative. Isaiah has not time to revel in his private emotions. He is not concerned with re-imagining God! Rather, only when his sin, seen in all its massive and objective reality, is removed can Isaiah hear the voice of God. 'Whom shall I send and who will go for us?'[10]

As God reveals himself to His people through Word and Sacrament in their worship – this is a reminder to firmly ensure the Lord is the central focus and object of their worship. Even though we may have ecstatic and memorable experiences as the Lord ministers to us – we are not to make ourselves and our subjective feelings the quintessence of worship.

## EZEKIEL'S VISION OF WORSHIP

Those called by the Lord in the Old Testament to be a prophet usually made one of two responses. Moses and Jeremiah classically protested their suitability for the task –

not that the Lord was going to be so easily rebuffed and take 'no' for an answer. Their resistance was countered by the persistent summons of the Lord. In contrast Isaiah and Ezekiel were constrained to respond to the supernatural nature of their call. Ezekiel the son of Buzi a priest was himself training as a priest. When he was younger he lived through the exciting days of the reforms of Josiah. Days when Jeremiah begun his preaching and prophetic ministry. W. Eichrodt says: 'Ezekiel must have been profoundly impressed by the religious aspects of the reform as he saw the temple being cleansed of the heathen filth that had settled in it, and the original forms and laws of Yahweh for worship being put into force. This must have aroused his enthusiasm at the thought of the greatness of the task that this would lay upon the shoulders of the temple priesthood. The renewal of the covenant between Israel and her God, sworn to by king and people in a solemn act of state must have seemed to bring back the ideal period of David.'[11]

Unfortunately, Josiah the King was killed in 609 BC and his reign and reforms ended abruptly. As was predicted by Jeremiah Jerusalem was defeated by a foe from the North, Nebuchadnezzar in 597 BC, when he deported around 10,000 of the population. Ezekiel was among the exiles taken to Babylon and the aspiration of being a priest in the temple in Jerusalem was devastatingly snatched away from him. In exile the elders could order their own affairs and were able to continue worshipping the Lord but this was limited as there was no temple. It is quite likely that many of the priests were also among the exiles.

D. Block points out that for Ezekiel the exile of Jehoiachin the king, along with his own deportation probably meant the end of all his professional dreams. The use of the first person in 33: 21 and 40:1 suggests that he was among the thousands of soldiers, craftspeople and nobility who had been sent into exile along with the king. They were the victims of a common ancient Near Eastern policy toward conquered peoples: the mass deportation of entire populations designed to break down national resistance at home by removing political and spiritual leadership, and to bolster the economy and military machine of the conqueror's homeland.[12]

Five long years after he had been in exile the Lord revealed himself to Ezekiel in his visions. These visions not only authenticated his call as a prophet, they also confirmed the strident nature of God's word that he was called to speak to his own people in exile. As you read the early chapters of Ezekiel you almost recoil at the difficult nature of what the Lord summoned him to say and do as a prophet. Through these visions the Lord spoke powerfully into his life – and without them it is unlikely he would have had the assurance and courage to do what the Lord asked him.

Blenkinsopp raises the possibility Ezekiel was ordained priest in exile and that the 'mysterious divine glory which appeared to him was also thought to appear at the climax of the ordination service (Lev. 9: 6). So it is possible he was called to be a prophet in the same year in which he was ordained priest – perhaps during the act of worship accompanying the ordination. In what follows there is at any rate a clear connection with worship. The description of the divine throne is reminiscent of Isaiah's vision of a heavenly liturgy of which temple worship was the earthly counterpart.'[13]

In this context Ezekiel's vision of the glory of God is doubly striking, because it propelled him into a ministry that came completely out of the blue – one he had never entertained, nor consciously trained for. Having been born into a priestly family in Jerusalem his education from an early age evolved around his training to be a priest. We see from the book of Ezekiel that he was familiar with Israel's history and religious traditions. His theology embraced a worldview with God as the center – and his life as a priest also evolved around the things of God. C. Wright points out that 'few matched the sheer uncompromising singularity of Ezekiel's passion for Yahweh. Everything in his life and understanding was dominated by the attributes of Yahweh as God – especially the glory of God. We can trace his passion to the vision by the Kebar Canal when he was overwhelmed by the appearance of the likeness of the glory of the Lord. When God called Ezekiel through this extraordinary vision and transformed him – he had a powerful impact on a life and an intellect already thoroughly shaped by the centrality of Yahweh.'[14]

Although Ezekiel's training to be a priest had been woven into his entire life, at the age of thirty he was an exile in a foreign land with no hope whatsoever of starting his ministry as a priest in Jerusalem. At times his disappointment and sense of loss must have been acute. He probably felt the Lord had let him down and on occasions he may have questioned why the Lord hadn't intervened, so that he was not deported – and had He done so he could have begun his ministry as a priest in the temple. His call and identity were inextricably bound up with being a priest but now he had somewhat lost his sense of purpose. Being at ease and at peace with himself had also proved elusive – having been torn away from what his heart and soul was destined. W. Eichrodt also captures how Ezekiel probably felt as an exile:

> He was far from Yahweh's presence in the sanctuary (Jerusalem) – leading a shadowy existence in a lost world where there was not even the faintest glimmer of hope of liberation: all that must have weighed heavily upon the heart of the young priest...There in that unclean land there was nothing to hope for and no improvement could be effected. Jerusalem was the only place from which any light came...So the young

priest had to pass though a waiting period of
agonising tension in which hope and fear alternated.[15]

Wright also draws our attention to how traumatic it must
have been for Ezekiel who was trained as a priest to
suddenly find himself called to be a prophet.'The disjunction
between the two was both theological and professional.
While we can see the benefits his training as a priest brought
to bear on his prophetic ministry we should not overlook
the immense personal, professional and theological shock it
must have been to Ezekiel, when at the age of thirty when he
was eligible to be ordained a priest in Jerusalem, God broke
into his life and wrecked all such career prospects and
constrained him into a role that he had never previously
entertained.

> No wonder the anger and bitter rage to which he
> honestly confesses disorientated and overwhelmed
> him for a full week – 3: 14-15. God would use all that
> he had built into Ezekiel's life during his years
> of preparation, but he would use it in radically
> different ways from anything he had ever imagined.
> Such is sometimes the way of God with those whom
> he calls to his service.[16]

## THE GLORY OF GOD

> In the thirtieth year, in the fourth month, on the fifth
> day of the week as I was among the exiles by the
> river Cebar, the heavens opened and I saw visions of
> God.
>
> Over the heads of the living creatures there was the
> likeness of a firmament, shining like a crystal spread
> out above their heads. And under the firmament their
> wings were stretched out straight one toward another:
> and each creature had two wings covering its body.
> And when they went I heard the sound of their wings

like the sound of many waters, like the thunder of the
Almighty, a sound of tumult like the sound of a host:
when they stood still they let down their wings. And
their came a voice from above the firmament over
their heads: when they stood still they let down their
wings. And above the firmament over their heads was
the likeness of a throne, in appearance like sapphire
and seated above the likeness of a throne was a
likeness as it were of a human form. And upward
from what had the appearance of his loins I saw as
it were gleaming bronze, like the appearance of a
closed fire and there was brightness round about him.
Like the appearance of a bow that is in the cloud
on the day of rain, so was the appearance of the
brightness round about.

Such was the appearance of the likeness of the glory
of the Lord. And when I saw it I fell on my face and I
heard the voice of one speaking.  Eze. 1: 1, 22-28

Although the word worship is not specifically used, the
scene portrayed around the throne of God pulsates with
divine worship. In the climax of Ezekiel's vision a vast
crystal expanse sparkled with awesome brightness. Through
and above this transparent crystal he saw a throne in a
brilliant rich blue, constructed from one of the most precious
stones of the ancient world – lapis lazuli. And on the throne
with all the added brilliance of contrasting fiery amber was
a figure like that of a man. 'His vision involves fascinating
reversal of the concept of 'image of God...Here in
anthropomorphic reversal God appears in the likeness of
a human being – albeit in glowing fiery splendour that
anticipates the transfiguration of the incarnate Son of God
himself and certainly provided the imagery for John's great
vision of the heavenly throne in Revelation 4...This is none
other than Yahweh himself very much alive and still on the

throne…Nothing will ever be more significant for Ezekiel than this encounter with the living God.'[17]

Lying prostrate captures Ezekiel's involuntary response of worship to the revelation of God's glory. Wright perceives that God's glory reveals His transcendence and the cosmic exaltation of the Lord pervades the worship of Israel – and he warns worshippers against any 'chummy familiarity.' The glory of the Lord also reveals His sovereignty and the image of a throne itself speaks of authority and power. It also manifests God's omnipresence because of the very location of the vision. God has arrived in Babylon in all his glory.[18] The vision of the Lord – a vision of divine heavenly realities announces from God's perspective the reality of things as they are on earth and transforms Ezekiel. The Lord has taken the initiative to reveal that He is God and that He is in control of human history. Ezekiel has had the eyes of his heart enlightened beyond belief and beyond imagination. What he has seen speaks into the very depths of his soul even though no words are initially uttered.

This vision is a reminder that Paul prays for the Ephesian Christians to have 'the eyes of their hearts enlightened' and is a call to us to offer up the same prayer for the Church. He prayed that the Lord would give them a revelation to grasp and perceive, to see and to understand spiritual truths. Such revelation from the Lord transcends intellectual comprehension and fills our hearts so they overflow with God's glory. It is a prayer for God to fill our hearts with himself and who He is – so that the Lord who dwells on the throne and is high and lifted up, will also reign in our hearts in all His glory. It can also be a prayer for God to inhabit our worship and fill it with himself and who He is – so that the Lord who dwells on His throne and is high and lifted up, will also reign in our worship.

## A SUPERNATURAL VISION

In Ezekiel's vision Block understands the significance of
the supernatural creatures who had four faces, one of which
was like a man's face. He points out that while to a modern
reader the choice of animals in the vision may seem arbitrary
they were a natural choice, as they frequently appear on
ancient iconographic and glyptic art and for Israel they
also had symbolic significance. The lion was renowned for
its courage, ferocity and strength and also served as a symbol
of royalty. The eagle was the swiftest and most stately
of birds. The ox was a symbol of fertility and divinity. 'In
the absence of abstract philosophical tools these images
expressed the transcendent divine attributes of omnipotence
and omniscience. Carrying the divine throne, the four-headed
cherubim declare that Yahweh has the strength and majesty
of the lion, the swiftness and mobility of the eagle, the
procreative power of the bull, and the wisdom and reason of
humankind.'[19]

The wheels in Ezekiel's vision symbolise some sort of
four-wheeled chariot and their ability to move in any
direction. Their magnificent wheels gleamed with the
brilliance of beryl and their rims full of eyes represented the
all-seeing, all-knowing character of God. The movement of
the wheels was perfectly synchronised with those of the
creatures, and the harmony between them is attributed to
the 'spirit of life' (*ruach hahayya*) – denoting the life giving
energising power of God. 'It was this energising spirit that
also determined the direction and freedom of movement of
the heavenly vehicle.'[20]

Ezekiel saw that above the heads of the creatures they
appeared to be holding up a sparkling platform, above which
was the likeness of a throne and seated above the throne
was the likeness as it were of a human form. The wings of
the creatures made a noise like the sound of many waters,
like the thunder of the Almighty, a sound of tumult like the

sound of a host. These loud sounds may be reminiscent of Yahweh's appearance to Israel on Mt. Sinai that was accompanied by peals of thunder. Block concludes this section (v. 22-28) by indicating that Ezekiel has finally caught onto the significance of the vision:

> This is none other than the glory of Yahweh. The doors of heaven have been flung wide open and he beholds Yahweh in all his splendour, enthroned above the living creatures. The term '*kabod*' derives from a root meaning 'to be heavy' but when applied to royalty and divinity it denotes the sheer weight of that person's majesty, that quality which evokes a response of awe in the observer. The prophet has witnessed the incredible – far away from the temple, among the exiles in the pagan land of Babylon, Yahweh has appeared to him. Ezekiel responds by appropriately falling down on his face in worship.[21]

No vision in the Old Testament matches the supernatural impact of the theophany of Ezekiel's vision. It has profound theological significance for a number of reasons. Everything in his vision proclaims the transcendent glory of God – a supernatural glory beyond our imagination. His vision also emanates with God's holiness and His sovereignty that are symbolised through God's elevation on His throne. The essence of Ezekiel's vision embraces God's immanence as he revealed His presence in the likeness of human form in the midst of His people in exile.

Block ends this section on Ezekiel's vision with a challenging note. 'This vision serves notice that whoever would enter into divine service must have a clear vision of the One into whose service he is called. The ministry is a vocation like no other: it

represents conscription into the service of the King of kings and Lord of lords – the One who sits on his glorious throne, unrivalled in majesty and power.'[22]
Anyone who would serve the Lord faces the challenge of a life altogether consumed  by being a worshipper of Yahweh.

## JOHN'S VISION OF WORSHIP

The author of Revelation modestly refers to himself as: 'I John your brother' – Rev.1: 9 rather than I John the beloved apostle although he had every right to. He does not pull rank on these Christians or elevate himself above them, as he feels no need to assert his authority. The churches he was writing to knew him and were familiar with his unassuming character. His humility reflects that as an apostle he had witnessed first hand Jesus' humility when he washed the disciples' feet.

'The early church generally accepted John the beloved disciple was the author of Revelation. This was confirmed as early as 150 AD by Justin Martyr and around 200 AD by Irenaeus and its apostolic authority was widely accepted by the ancient fathers.  From the style of writing we can discern that the author was a Hebrew who was very familiar with the Old Testament. While the language of the fourth Gospel is smooth and fluent and couched in accurate and simple Greek, that of Revelation is rough and harsh with many grammatical and syntactical irregularities. We can account for this difference as a disciple of John may have acted as a secretary to write the Gospel, while John himself wrote Revelation and his exile establishes the fact of persecution.'[23]

By way of reminder the letter is the revelation of Jesus Christ which God gave him to show what must soon take place: and he made it known by sending his angel to his servant John – Rev. 1: 1. It is worth bearing in mind that Revelation was written to be read out as a pastoral letter, to the churches in Asia, to the congregations who knew John personally. He may have intended it be read during a Communion Service as there is a specific allusion to the messianic banquet throughout the book. Also the concluding lines in ch. 22 form something of a transition to the eucharistic celebration. As we read it, it is important to bear in mind the original audience and how they would have understood it.[24] But Revelation also highlights that 'one of the most important things that worship accomplishes is to remind us that we worship not merely as a congregation or a church, but as part of the church, the people of God. John reminds his readers that their worship is a participation in the unceasing celestial praise of God. So too, the worship of God's people today finds its place in the 'middle' of a throng representing every people and nation and tribe and tongue.'[25]

### REVELATION 4: 2-11

At once I was in the Spirit and lo a throne stood in heaven with one seated on the throne. And he who sat there appeared like jasper and carnelian and round the throne was a rainbow that looked like an emerald. Round the throne there were twenty-four thrones and seated on the thrones were twenty-four elders, clad in white garments with golden crowns on their heads. From the throne issue flashes of lightning and voices of peals of thunder, and before the throne burn seven torches of fire which are the seven spirits of God: and before the throne there is as it were a sea of glass like crystal.

And round the throne on each side of the throne are four living creatures, full of eyes in front and behind: the first living creature like a lion, the second living creature like an ox, the third living creature with the face of a man and the fourth living creature like a flying eagle. And the four living creatures each of them with six wings, are full of eyes all round and within, and day and night they never cease to sing:

> Holy, holy, holy, is the Lord God Almighty –
> Who was and is and is to come!

And whenever the living creatures give glory and honour and thanks to him who is seated on the throne, who lives for ever and ever – the twenty-four elders fall down before him who is seated on the throne and worship him who lives for ever and ever: they cast their crowns before the throne singing.

> Worthy art thou, our Lord and God to
> receive glory and honour and power:
> for thou didst create all things
> and by thy will they were created.

The apocalypse of John draws aside the invisible curtain that restricts our view of the heavenly realm – a drawing back that reveals the world in a radically new light. His vision of heaven takes him into the throne room of the universe where God rules over all earthly matters and from which emanates ultimate authority and power. Here his eyes are also opened to the worship in the heavenly places around the throne of God that is never ending.

Aspects of Revelation are thought to reflect Ezekiel's vision of God's throne and Isaiah's earlier temple vision. Whereas Ezekiel describes what seemed like a human form seated above the throne – 'as the appearance of the likeness of the glory of God' – John's figure on the throne has an appearance similar to jasper and carnelian. Ian Boxall says:

> The use of precious stones in John's description evokes the dazzling splendour of the divine adoration and worship. So too does the emerald which is used to describe the rainbow encircling the throne…

Elsewhere in Revelation jasper will describe the radiance of God's holy city and its wall (21: 11, 18). While all three jewels will be found in the city's foundations (21: 19). In Jewish tradition they are among the jewels on the high priest's breastplate (Ex. 28: 17-20).[26]

The reference to an emerald like a rainbow in John's vision displays the magnificence of the heavenly scene. As we view the throne of God and the heavenly court around it, we have a glimpse of the transcendent beauty and awe-inspiring worship that takes place there.

In John's vision there are twenty-four thrones with twenty four-elders seated on them who are identified as exalted human beings, dressed in shining white garments with crowns upon their heads – which may indicate priestly and royal functions, although their garments are also reminiscent of those worn by angels. Boxall says: 'In short the twenty-four elders are almost certainly the angelic heavenly personification of the people of God. Their presence here close to the divine throne serves as an assurance to the vulnerable but faithful among the seven churches (Rev. 1-3), that the promises made to them by the son of man figure will indeed come to fruition. As in heaven so ultimately on earth.'[27] At the heart of this vision is the eye-catching phenomena that emanate from the throne of God – flashes of lightning, voices and peals of thunder. These awesome sounds are reminiscent of the theophany that accompanied God's glory and presence at Mt. Sinai (Ex. 19: 16-18) following the deliverance of His people from Egypt. 'At strategic points throughout Revelation similar phonomena will recur with increasing intensity, as God acts again with judgment to overcome injustice and save His people (8: 5, 11: 19, 16: 18).[28]

The four living creatures in John's vision resemble those in Ezekiel's and Isaiah's visions and here they are immersed in divine worship day and night, every day, without ceasing. Ladd says: 'It is quite clear that these four living creatures are analogous to the Seraphim of Is. 6: 1-3 and the cherubim of Ezek. 10: 14...Either the cherubim represent the praise and adoration extended to the Creator by the totality of his creation: or else they represent angelic beings who are used by the Creator in exercising his rule and his divine will in all the orders of his creation.'[29] The first part of their canticle is the same as Isaiah's as they unequivocally declare that God is holy. Their continual worship is complemented by that of the elders in a series of concentric circles around the throne of the Holy One. 'But theirs is no merely cerebral activity of speaking or singing. They fall down in front of the one seated on the throne in a gesture of divine worship, casting their golden wreaths before the throne. It may be that such a ritual parodies practice in the imperial court, where senators and representatives of the provincial cities presented the emperor with golden crowns on specific occasions. It is not the emperor but the Holy One seated on the authentic throne who deserves such honours.

> This vision is a salutary reminder that the rather cerebral activity which often passes for religious worship, would have been unrecognisable as such in the ancient world and certainly finds no support in the Apocalypse. Here the worship of heaven is an activity which involves the whole person and all the human senses: speech: sight: hearing: touch and even smell.'[30]

### WORSHIPPING THE LAMB

And between the throne and the four living creatures and among the elders, I saw a Lamb standing as though it had been slain, with seven horns and with seven eyes which are the seven spirits of God sent

out into all the earth: and he went and took the scroll
from the right hand of him who was seated on
the throne. And when he had taken the scroll the
our living creatures and the twenty-four elders fell
down before the Lamb, each holding a harp and with
golden bowls of incense which are the prayers of the
saints: and they sang a new song saying:

'Worthy art thou to take the scroll and to open it seals
for thou wast slain and by thy blood didst ransom
men for God, from every tribe and tongue and people
and nation, and hast made them a kingdom and
priests to our God, and they shall reign on earth.'

Then I looked and I heard around the throne and the
living creatures and the elders the voice of many
angels, numbering myriads of myriads and thousands
of thousands, saying with a loud voice: 'Worthy is
the Lamb who was slain, to receive power and wealth
and wisdom and might and honour and glory
and blessing!' And I heard every creature in heaven
and on earth and under the earth and in the sea and
all therein saying: 'To him who sits upon the throne
and to the Lamb be blessing and honour and glory
and might for ever and ever!' And the four living
creatures said: 'Amen!' and the elders fell down and
worshipped. Rev. 5: 6-14

In John's vision the Lamb now replaces the allusion to
Jesus as 'someone like a son of man' and is the central
Christological title (this occurs 28 times in Rev.). Chapter 5
opens with a very moving scene that culminates in Jesus
the Lamb being worthy to open the scroll  (the significance
of this is revealed in the following chapters) because of
his death on the cross: and because his blood ransomed
people for God from every tribe and nation. This is the
enthronement of the Lamb and the worship of Jesus the

Lamb reflects the worship that took place in ch. 4. The heavenly creatures who have a harp and golden bowls of incense, is reminiscent of the worship in the temple at Jerusalem. A reminder that the 'earthly liturgy of both the Tabernacle and the Temple was patterned upon the true heavenly sanctuary.'[31]

John's vision bursts into a panoramic scene of worship of unrivalled splendour when he describes the angelic host as a countless multitude. 'The angelic liturgy is impressive indeed in it scale and intensity. These lesser angels also sing a canticle which proclaims that the Lamb is worthy...As this vision reaches its climax with ear-splitting intensity the whole of creation is caught up in the praise of God and the Lamb...We catch a glimpse here of what creation was intended for and what can in God's great plan be on earth, as it is in heaven. God and the Lamb hitherto addressed separately are now acclaimed together in one great concluding doxology – the objects of praise and honour, glory and strength, for ever and ever...Then the elders fall down before the throne and the Lamb, in a posture of silent and profound worship.'[32]

The worship of God and Jesus the Lamb that takes place in heaven, is in an atmosphere that is profoundly moving as the elders fall down and worship. The posture of falling down – lying prostrate on the floor is evocative of total submission in worship to God and Christ. Christians in the Orthodox Churches do prostrate themselves in worship – and it may be timely to provide the opportunity for God's people in the West to also prostrate themselves as an act of worship to the Lord in the sanctuary. Matt Redman calls this 'face down worship.' I believe this act of worship can powerfully symbolise lives yielded to the Lordship of Christ.

## WORSHIP – CONFLICT & VICTORY

After this I heard what seemed to be the voice of a great multitude in heaven crying: 'Hallelujah! Salvation and glory and power belong to our God, for his judgments are true and just: he has judged the great harlot who corrupted the earth with her fornication, and he has avenged on her the blood of his servants.' Once more they cried: 'Hallelujah! The smoke from her goes up for ever and ever.' And the twenty-four elders and the four living creatures fell down and worshipped God who is seated on the throne saying: 'Amen. Hallelujah!' And from the throne came a voice saying crying: 'Praise God all you his servants, you who fear him, small and great.' Then I heard what seemed like the voice of a great multitude, like the sound of many waters and like the sound of mighty thunderpeals crying: 'Hallelujah for the Lord our God the Almighty reigns. Let us rejoice and exult and give him the glory, for the marriage of the Lamb has come and his bride has made herself ready: it was granted to her to be clothed with fine linen, bright and pure – for the fine linen is the righteous deeds of the saints. Rev. 19. 1-9

Rev. ch. 18 announces the fall of Babylon and opens our eyes to the invisible spiritual powers that are opposed to God's kingdom. When John wrote to the seven churches Rome would have been seen as Babylon. Now in the 21st century it may represent a power that seeks to establish control and dominion over peoples' lives. In Rev. ch. 12 and 13 we also read of a dragon and a beast being worshipped by men. These disturbing chapters introduce us to an underlying theme in Revelation that takes place on earth involving 'worship and conflict.'

Noel Due in 'Created For Worship' echoes this theme when he says: 'Behind the scenes of history lie spiritual powers, unveiled in the book of Revelation for what they really are. The principle of their operation is imitative in that they seek to set up a counterfeit to the reality of God and his purposes. 'The red dragon who is Satan has the incarnation of his 'son' in the beast who is the counterpart of Christ, i.e. who is the antichrist. He has a 'death' and 'resurrection' (Rev. 13: 3) and the power of his death and resurrection is to make all men worship the beast. The second beast who is the false prophet the evil counterpart of the Holy Spirit causes humanity to worship the image of the beast: and the beast is in collusion with the unholy woman, Babylon, who is the foul counterpart of the pure Bride the church of Christ.'[33]

In Rev. ch 19 in the throne room of heaven true worship pervades the atmosphere, where the victory of Christ over evil results in resounding liturgical praise, in a canticle involving heavenly worshippers. The shout of 'Halellujah' resounds four times in six verses and occurs only in the New Testament in Revelation. Once again the twenty-four elders and the four creatures fall down and worship God. This heavenly liturgy is resplendent with the choral singing of a vast multitude of worshippers. They rejoice in God's salvation and final victory over evil and also rejoice in His justice and in His Kingly rule. The ecstatic worship of the angelic hallelujah chorus, the elders and the creatures ushers in the second coming of the marriage of the Lamb with his Bride, the Church. This is a scene of great celebration, rejoicing and triumph. E. Boring says:

> Even with all the language of judgment the scene never ceases to be a worship scene. The smoke of Babylon that ascends forever is only a grisly contrast to the incense of heavenly worship. Worship celebrates 'the mighty acts of God' not our pious feelings...Worship is the dominating note of the concluding scene of this vision.[34]

# CHAPTER SIX
# CONTEMPORARY & CHARISMATIC WORSHIP

## INTRODUCTION

Exactly what is it that qualifies someone to write about contemporary and charismatic worship? It seems reasonable to assume the author will be familiar with these styles of worship and have first hand experience of them. We also expect him to show an awareness of what other writers have to say. We trust that he will be theologically literate and able to reflect theologically about worship. We look to him to show that he is familiar with biblical principles of worship to inform this topic. We hope that he will affirm the positive things about these styles of worship, but will not be at all surprised if challenging questions are raised about them. Some of these might be controversial but others enable us to think about worship on a deeper level.

In this context I share my experience of contemporary and charismatic worship. I also document the history of these two styles of worship along with what other authors have to say about them. And I share some individuals' experience of them as this helps us to understand how they can evolve.

In 1977 two Greek friends invited me to go with them and a group from their Baptist Church to a Christian holiday at Ashburnham in Sussex. This was run by the Fountain Trust where Tom Smail was the speaker. If they had told me this was a charismatic holiday this would have meant absolutely nothing to me. This was my first experience of charismatic worship. Essentially it consisted of worship songs punctuated by a sermon followed by more songs. There was one particular evening that stood out because the presence of the Lord was so real. The worship began at 8 pm and at 10 pm Tom Smail apologised that we had to stop because the coffee was ready. My reaction was who wants to stop worshipping when the presence of the Lord is so real and tangible?

In the years that followed the Lord brought me into contact with other charismatic churches and denominations. I went to the Dales at the beginning of the 1980s where Bryn Jones was the leader and speaker. The first evening we were part of 3,000 people who were enthusiastically worshipping the Lord in the most exuberant manner. The style of celebratory worship was rather overwhelming but we adjusted to it the next day. One astonishing thing took place at the Dales. They had an Old Testament 'heap (heave?) offering' because they wanted to raise around £33,000 to pay for new sound recording equipment. The next evening it was announced that £250,000 had been given or pledged, with one person giving a house worth £35,000. These charismatic Christians not only knew how to worship joyfully but also how to give generously too.

During the middle of the 80's when I was a theological student at St. John's College in Nottingham, I was part of a city center student church, St. Nick's, that embraced the teaching of John Wimber. Also between 86-87 I was on placement as a student at St. Margaret's Church in Aspley in Nottingham. A few years earlier the church had experienced charismatic renewal but due to a change in leadership this was not sustained. As I got to know people I perceived this was a cause of great disappointment to those who had been involved. As it turned out the vicar was not able to lead them deeper into renewal so that this matured. As we shall see later, from Tom Smail's comments, this is a fairly common occurrence for those who experience charismatic renewal.

On occasions I also worshipped with my wife Sarah at The Assemblies Of God in Talbot Street in Nottingham (a Pentecostal Church) as her cousin worshipped there. Here the service consisted of 45 minutes of worship, the notices and then a 45 minute sermon. I was impressed by the fact that every Friday night between 8–12 pm they had a half night of prayer for their church and the city. Attendance on Sunday morning was around 300 and later when they moved to a warehouse it was around 500. In their sung worship that lasted 45 minutes there was a tangible awareness of the presence of the Lord. Yet this seemed to pass quickly and there was a sense of being in a dimension where time stood still. When you are worshipping in the presence of the Lord time goes out of the window. St. Thomas Crook's in Sheffield is the only Anglican Church I have been to (in the mid 80s) where there was the same heightened awareness of the presence of the Lord.

Over the years I have heard Colin Urquart speak (a well known Anglican charismatic leader), visited Spring Harvest and St. Andrew's Chorleywood when Bishop David Pytches was the Vicar. Towards the end of the 90s I also visited two churches where the Toronto Blessing had arrived. This was the latest wave of charismatic renewal to come to Britain and it originated at the Toronto Airport Vineyard Fellowship. It was accompanied by various signs such as laughter and people falling down, commonly referred to as 'slain in the Spirit.' Although this movement caused some controversy many testified to experiencing a real love for Christ. My first curacy in 1988 was in an Anglican Evangelical charismatic church who were a spiritually gifted fellowship. Although not everyone identified themselves as charismatic, for those who did they believed in baptism in the Holy Spirit and the use of spiritual gifts. St. Barnabas an Anglican church in Cambridge where I now worship also describes itself as Evangelical charismatic. This is an eclectic church with a relatively young congregation predominantly under 40. It is privilege and a tremendous sight to see so many young people worshipping when the membership of many Anglican churches is often considerably older.

## CONTEMPORARY WORSHIP

By implication the term contemporary suggests something that is modern and state of the art. The latest innovation in any particular field we are talking about. Contemporary worship could be perceived as taking place in a church that has been modernised and de-cluttered of pews installed in the 20th century or earlier. A place of worship furnished with comfortable chairs, modern lighting and modern furniture in the sanctuary. The term contemporary suggests creativity and innovation in worship and may well include the use of the latest presentational technologies, that enable people to project still and moving images from song lyrics to video clips on a screen. 'High-tech worship relies extensively on computer-based presentational technologies, from still and animated slides created in programs like Power-Point to video recordings and live video projection piped to screens in the sanctuary.'[1]

Q. J. Schultze astutely perceives the key to the wise use of presentational technologies is not use for their own sake. He believes technology tends to create hearts and minds bent on control and manufactures worship in tune with mere human desires. In contrast worship calls us to remember ultimately who is in control, as worship is a God-sanctioned activity not a human creation.

> When we fail to see technology within the context of the power, majesty and glory of God, we can become more enchanted with our technological ability that we are humbled by God's grace. We wrongly focus on our liturgical accomplishments on our technological skills and apparent power, rather than on what God has done for us and is doing.

He also raises the issue of how the role of presentational technologies can enable us to dialogue with God, as worship is a response to God. Hence worship becomes a drama of a dialogue with God.[2]

Contemporary worship can refer to a 'movement and a style of worship that focuses on the culturally accessible and relevant, on the new and innovative, on the use of recent technologies of communication…At its heart is the attempt to relate to God and praise God in the language of the people. As that language changes so does the style – but not the substance and center of worship.'[3] T. & R. Wright also believe the Contemporary Worship Movement uses the style and language of secular people to communicate the truth of the gospel to them. It also seeks to remove some of the barriers of religious language that keeps people from church.[4]

Contemporary worship may also be understood in terms of the modern songs we sing. This often includes songs that are two to three decades old although they are complemented with a regular stream of new ones. For instance, an Anglican Service of the Word, can still include contemporary songs with a cluster of songs together. Or such a service may have two clusters of sung worship. This is often called a 'time of worship' which can be seen as the real time of worship. As sung worship along with the preaching can be perceived as the main events, there is little for the worshipper to know about the dynamics, the flow and the theology of worship.

In this genre of worship no longer is the sanctuary-stage likely to be defined as a 'sacred space' with a cross on the communion table as the central focus. Instead this may well resemble a concert stage with the musicians and their instruments dominating the scene. The minister may not wear a clerical collar and the leadership style and atmosphere is likely to be informal – in an attempt to be culturally relevant and accessible, however that may be interpreted. Informality coupled with the desire for intimacy, may claim to aim for the immanence of God in worship – but can result in the loss of His transcendence.

In 'Discerning The Spirit,' Plantinga Jr. & Rozeboom share that to more classically minded Christians, this style of worship represents the blowing not of the Spirit of God but of the spirit of the age. These Christians believe the church has sold its soul and worship seems less like the company of the saints and martyrs than like a nightclub that forgot to close. So they wonder: 'Why present the Gospel in an ethos that clashes with it? Why stand for worldly entertainment rather than against it?'[5] While this may sound like a caricature it does force us to reflect whether the ethos of contemporary worship, reduces God to the immediacy of cultural convenience and fashionable trends.

In contemporary and charismatic worship there is likely to be a band of musicians who almost certainly play loud music. The terms 'contemporary' and 'charismatic' worship might be used interchangeably, although they describe different styles. It is not unusual to find churches who describe themselves as charismatic but whose worship in reality is only contemporary. Authentic charismatic worship not only regularly makes space for members to use their spiritual gifts, time is also made to listen to God speak through the Holy Spirit – as we find in Acts 13. Such churches are also open to the Lord ministering to them in the power of the Spirit and this calls for spiritual discernment by those leading worship.

## THE ROOTS OF PRAISE & WORSHIP

The 60s and 70s saw an increase in the songbooks churches began to use. From those heady days of Youth Praise in the 60s evolved new songbooks such as Mission Praise, Songs Of Fellowship, Spring Harvest, Graham Kendrick, Hosanna – The Vineyard and Soul Survivor. They all contributed contemporary praise and worship songs in their respective eras. Evangelicals usually see praise as an element of worship along with adoration, thanksgiving and confession. But for charismatics praise and worship signify a flow and progression in the service from the joyful and noisy songs to the quieter more worshipful song. Psalm 95 is an example of this transition where the atmosphere changes form praising the Lord to worshipping Him.

Worship that includes contemporary songs has its roots in the House Church Movement and in Christian holidays like Spring Harvest and latterly New Wine and Soul Survivor. Those older than the 20-30s age group will have deeper roots in contemporary worship than in such festivals as New Wine and Soul Survivor. When Spring Harvest began in 1979, 3,000 people attended in Prestatyn North Wales. By 1987 this had increased to 50,000 and by 1990 the number attending was 80,000. Pete Ward says: 'Central to the impact of S. H. was the way that the event spread charismatic styles of worship around the country...With these changes also came a shift in fortunes within the charismatic movement. Walker argues that the success of S. H. is one of the main reasons for what he sees as the decline in the 'Restoration' group of churches...Through S. H. individual Christians were able to experience a similar excitement and style of worship to that which was on offer at the Restorationist Dales and Downs Bible weeks. At S. H. however, they were able to do so without taking on board the restrictive authority structure.'[6]

### THE RESTORATION MOVEMENT

James Steven informs us that the Restoration Movement was originally part of the Charismatic Movement in the 60s. But in the 70s it began to take on its own distinctive characteristics as the Charismatic Movement then diverged into two main streams – Renewal and Restorationism. Those in the Renewal Movement focused in The Fountain Trust, sought to live out the implications of charismatic life within the established church institutions (Anglican, Catholic & Methodist churches). The Restoration Movement sought to go further in radically altering church structures according to their perception of biblical principles. The majority of its members had their roots in the Independent, Free Church tradition (Brethren, Independent Baptist, Evangelical Free Church, Assemblies of God) and they were used to the concept of local autonomy.

In the early 70s many of the small house church fellowships began to order themselves in larger network fellowships, such as New Frontiers led by Terry Virgo, the Pioneer Trust led by Gerald Coates and Ichthus led by Roger Forster. The song-writers Graham Kendrick (Ichthus Fellowship London) and Dave Fellingham (Clarendon Church Hove) are associated with this movement. The style of their services essentially consists in worship lasting up to 45 minutes, followed by the notices and then a sermon also lasting up to 45 minutes. This includes an opportunity to respond either by standing so the pastor prays for them, or by coming up to the platform at the front to receive prayer individually.

The Restoration Movement exclusively adheres to the Bible in every aspect of church life and is Conservative Evangelicalism at its most fundamental. One of the other distinct aspects of its theology is 'Baptism in the Holy Spirit' –which is essential if Christians are to have power to witness and be effective in prayer and minister in the realm of spiritual gifts. Andrew Walker calls the Restorationists a 'Kingdom people.' Many of their songs emphasise the sovereignty and majesty of God and the ascended Christ seated at the Father's right hand. This is matched by a corresponding sense of being 'kingdom people' and involves a thorough commitment to God's purposes of restoring the Kingdom. Another major emphasis of the Kingdom is a renewal of worship. Here Scripture controls the songs and there is an expectation that 'God will be in their midst.'[7]

## DYNAMICS OF CHARISMATIC WORSHIP

Robb Redman identifies the structure of charismatic worship by comparing the John Wimber, Vineyard Model with neo-Pentecostal practice. The Wimber model uses five distinct phases in free-flowing praise. * Invitation: * engagement: * exaltation: * adoration: * intimacy. He points out that in this model the first 3-5 songs are often upbeat and focus on gathering to worship God and then attending to the nature and attributes of God in exaltation. The music often shifts at this point to a softer, mellower sound to permit the worship to acknowledge God's presence in adoration. Thematically the adoration and intimacy sections feature songs that address God personally. The final intimacy phase is the quietest. In many Vineyard churches songs rich in biblical and non-biblical language predominate: many songs describe a relationship with God in physical terms – seeing, hearing, touching holding, kissing. As biblical justification for this Vineyard worship leaders emphasise a meaning of the New Testament Greek word for worship (*proskuneo*) 'to turn towards to kiss' which they take to mean intimacy or closeness to God.[8]

The neo-Pentecostal approach to worship similarly has a five-stage process and draws on an understanding of worship in the ancient Jewish tabernacle and temple. * Outside the camp: * through the gates with thanksgiving: * into his courts with praise: * onto the holy place: * into the holy of holies. The service begins with the gathering of the people outside the dwelling place of God, rejoicing in the encounter with God about to take place with upbeat and energetic songs. Psalm 100 is the cue for the next two stages: 'Enter His gates with thanksgiving and His courts with praise.' The songs celebrate the greatness of God and offer thanks for God's goodness. The mood changes as worshippers move into these two phases – 'all attention is now directed solely to God, Jesus or the Holy Spirit.'[9]

### JOHN WIMBER'S INFLUENCE

Contemporary worship owes an enormous debt of gratitude to the late John Wimber and the Vineyard Movement he founded. Therefore, it is appropriate to chart its history and contribution to worship. One major factor that influenced John was his background as a musician. As an only child he spent long hours alone and learned to play over twenty different musical instruments with his favourite being the saxophone. By the age of fifteen he was an accomplished musician. After graduating he embarked on a professional music career and in 1953 he won first prize at the Lighthouse International Jazz Festival. In 1962 he actually bought an up-and-coming group called the Righteous Brothers and played sax for them. In 1964 they released their hit single 'You've Lost That Loving Feeling.'[10]

I found it moving to learn about John's background as a musician. This undoubtedly was an influential factor in later years in Christian worship – although much of what he saw and did in the music business was contrary to his philosophy of worship. John passionately called his worship leaders to make 'Jesus famous' instead of promoting their own ministries. And he was turned off by anything that smacked of self-promotion or glitzy performance. He discouraged musical exhibitions that would steal the church's affection for Jesus if they drew attention to the worship leader or the band and believed worship leaders were servants. Simple pure devotion to Jesus was the outstanding trait of early Vineyard worship.[11]

It will probably surprise many people to discover that before he was the leader of the Vineyard Movement, John Wimber was the Pastor of a Quaker Church. Both he and his wife Carol were influenced by the Quakers' emphasis on waiting for the Lord and openness to the Holy Spirit.

The silent meeting for worship is the most visible element of classical Quaker worship. The worshippers assemble without leader or program, stilling their minds and focusing their attention waiting to sense the presence of God and then to respond as they are moved in their own spirits.[12]

Andy Park points out that John Wimber had a genuine desire to have deep communion with God in worship. He resisted any manipulative techniques that would cheapen the worship experience and make it fleshy rather than spiritual. God met John and Carol in their Quaker worship in a small group in 1977 which later became the Anaheim Vineyard. This is how Carol Wimber describes those early days.

We began worship with nothing but a sense of the calling from the Lord to a deeper relationship with Him. Before we started meeting in a small home church setting in 1977, the Holy Spirit had been working in my heart creating a tremendous hunger for God. One day as I was praying the word 'worship' appeared in my mind like a newspaper headline. I had never thought much about that word before.

After we started to meet in our home gathering we noticed times during the meeting – usually when we sang – in which we experienced God deeply. We sang many songs but mostly songs about worship or testimonies from one Christian to another. But occasionally we sang a song personally and intimately to Jesus – with lyrics like 'Jesus I love you.' Those types of songs both stirred and fed the hunger of God within me.[13]

In the early days Carol recalls learning to sing *to* Jesus *not* about him. 'We realised that often we would sing about worship yet we never actually worshipped – except when we accidentally stumbled onto intimate songs like – 'I love you Lord.' Ever since the Vineyard has placed an emphasis on singing to the Lord and their worship is characterised by simple songs of love and devotion. From this an intimate kind of worship evolved that has had an influence around the world. John felt that God entrusted the Vineyard with a gift of worship that would be imparted to other parts of God's church.[14]

While Vineyard worship has had a wide influence, John Leach a former Director of Anglican Renewal Ministries, writing towards the end of the 90s felt that their songs did not have the range of feel, colour and tempo as a selection of our songs. Here he is referring to the type of songs Spring Harvest used at their Easter Celebrations. He felt Vineyard lyrics that were simple and intimate to one worshipper, could be slushy and theologically bereft to another – especially if you have been singing them for forty-five minutes. He felt that while their music was good on adoration and love and there are at least two songs of celebration and joy – that is about it. 'Particularly noticeable by its absence is any hint of the victorious mood of many of our spiritual warfare songs such as – 'Let God arise' or 'For this purpose.' I feel this is a serious lack, one which seemed like a real missed opportunity at a recent Vineyard conference.'[15]

As I have looked at the ethos of Vineyard worship, Soul Survivor and contemporary worship, this has raised an unspoken yet important implication – churches may find they are not as successful in replicating these styles of worship. It is clear that John Wimber had a distinctive call to the style of worship that evolved as the Vineyard model. Equally, it is clear that Matt Redman's style of worship evolved from when he was a young teenage Christian seeking to express his love for the Lord. To replicate these styles of worship requires more than enthusiastic musicians playing loudly. We have to take into account their spiritual formation that evolves over a period of years, where their call and vision for worship is refined and matures. Of equal significance is the development of their relationship with the Lord as He moulds them and the ministry they are called to. Paul Oakley echoes this when he says: 'There was a time when God called me to lay down music indefinitely to pursue Him and know Him more. I just kept an acoustic guitar in my room just so I could worship with it. It was almost a full two years before I felt God say, 'Now is the time to pick it up again' – but those two years were critical and foundational.'[16]

This spiritual formation involves a deep consecration to serve the Lord and His people through worship. There are no short cuts to reproducing successful styles of worship that well known leaders have cultivated over many years. Learning to lead others in worship, acquiring the skills this calls for and the sensitivity to the Holy Spirit this requires, means being dedicated to continue learning about worship – and how to lead and release others as worshippers too.

### DISTINCTIVE CHARISMATIC FEATURES
Peter Hocken 'In Streams of Renewal' – which charts the origins and early development of the Charismatic Movement in Britain, highlights some of its distinguishing features that are also relevant to charismatic worship. It is not unusual for charismatics to become preoccupied with spiritual gifts and the manifestation of spiritual power that is associated with them. But he points out that such an assumption could easily lead to the conclusion, that the possession of these gifts is the central focus of the movement.

It is then worthy of note that the participants
constantly testify that the primary aspect of accession
to the sphere of spiritual gifts is a new quality in their
knowledge and experience of God...The changed
relationship to God experienced by those baptised
in the Spirit was described in a variety of ways,
illustrating a greater consciousness of the Trinitarian
nature of God. Some spoke of a conscious inflowing
of God. Some had a clear sense of the presence
of God and his glory, some an inner peace and
knowledge of God's love. There is a particular place
in the witness for the person of Jesus Christ, with
frequent mention being made of a new knowledge
and love of the Saviour.[17]

A distinctive feature of charismatic worship is a new
or renewed desire to praise God. 'This new capacity to
worship was often experienced in terms of a welling up
within one's heart as the work of the indwelling Holy Spirit.'
This is especially associated with receiving the gift of
tongues itself experienced as spontaneous praise. Equally
notable is a new capacity for hearing God speak. Hearing the
Lord speak is perceived to happen in a number of ways: by
receiving pictures or impressions, or words of knowledge or
wisdom.[18]

Hocken highlights another distinctive feature of the
charismatic dimension when he says:'Pentecostal experience
has consistently been seen in terms of empowering by the
Holy Spirit. Some began their search for the Holy Spirit
through realising the ineffectiveness of their ministry. All
who sought more of the Holy Spirit knew that the Spirit
comes with the power of God...some of those baptised in the
Spirit first experienced God's power in relation to their own
lives in inner healing or experienced God's power to heal
through their ministry.

But the power of the Spirit evidenced in the origins of the Charismatic Movement is not restricted to healing and can also be seen for instance, in evangelism...some revival minded Anglican Evangelicals such as those at Gillingham also clearly experienced this baptism as a powerful tool for effective evangelism among the un-churched. The Pastor of the Good Shepherd Mission in Bethnal Green testified:

> My own church has been turned upside down. Instead of table tennis it is the open-air meeting. In two summers we have proclaimed the gospel to over 6,000 people in East London. Before this blessing the young people would not go out into the open air, but now, praise God, there is a hunger for precious souls. 'To God be the glory great things He has done.'[19]

Hocken points out that the Charismatic Movement has a distinctive shape with baptism in the Spirit being a central experience. Evidence of this baptism is seen when a person exercises any of the spiritual gifts that are in 1 Corinthians. Another notable aspect is being endued with the Lord's authority, when preaching or ministering using spiritual gifts. 'However, two other distinguishing features are key to understanding the essence and impact of the Charismatic Movement. The first feature is the transforming power of the Holy Spirit in peoples' lives to bring salvation, deliverance and healing in instances where there is addiction or brokenness. The second feature of this 'transforming grace' brought a rich complex of blessings and:

> A new closeness to and love for Jesus Christ: a new joy and peace: a new capacity to praise God: a new desire to read the Scriptures: a new power for ministry and witness, a new confidence in God.'[20]

Michael Harper a former Director of The fountain Trust also shares his experience of baptism in the Spirit when he was a curate at All Souls Church, Langham Place.

> To my utter amazement I began to experience what St. Paul had prayed so many years before. I was 'filled with all the fullness of God' and had to ask God to stop giving me more – I could not take it. For a fortnight I found it impossible to sleep so filled was I at one moment with 'joy unspeakable and full of glory' – and then deep conviction of sin as the Holy Spirit revealed areas of my life and ministry which had not been under His sovereign control, and then wonderfully fresh revelations of truth in His word. I experienced as never before the love of God literally poured into my heart so that I loved people I have previously only just tolerated. I found liberty and power in my ministry I had never thought possible. The Bible came alive to me and for several months it was the only book I wanted to read. Prayer was a new experience of intimate communion with my Master and the element of worship which had been almost totally absent before became an important part of my devotional life.[21]

### SOUL SURVIVOR & THE HEART OF WORSHIP

Anyone who has attended the annual Soul Survivior Festival started by Mike Pilavachi will know that 'the heart of worship' represents their ethos. It is a key metaphor in the Survivor Songbook. There is a heart to worship that seeks to express the intimacy between the believer and the Lord. Pete Ward says

> This heart is located in acknowledging that worship is all about Jesus. Heart here relates to the essence of the deepest truth of worship. It is possible to drift from this 'heart' to be distracted even by worship

itself. We can make worship something that it should not be but this is a mistake because the pure, essential nature of worship relates to Jesus. This is its heart.[22]

In worship we can also seek the heart of God the Father. 'To approach God's heart is to experience the grace of God who gives and gives. This is the heart of the Father, the merciful graciousness of the Lord...Searching for God's heart is the response of one lover to another. God holds our heart in his hands and we are committed to seeking after Him.'[23] When speaking of the believer's heart Ward says: 'Pouring out the heart in worship comes through the closeness of the Lord. At the same time the worship of the believer is a demonstration of love for Jesus. Such worship itself may be said to bless the heart of Jesus. Worship in the secret place where Jesus and the believer share their intimate connection. In the song 'I'm giving you my heart' the believer surrenders themselves to God.'[24]

As a song-writer and worship leader Matt Redman is an influential figure amongst his contemporaries in terms of the style of worship songs we sing today. One of his best known songs is 'When The Music Fades.' The birth of this particular song has a prophetic dimension to it, as it challenges us to think about what we are doing as we worship. It also speaks about the heart of worship and says that when all is stripped away worship is all about Jesus. The birth of this song in 1977 is particularly interesting. The Soul Survivor congregation based in Watford began to experience problems and Mike Pilavachi the leader shares what happened. 'Instead of focusing on God the whole thing had become so cluttered, so concerned with details that everyone in the church – leaders and congregation alike – became distracted by the worship. Was it Redman's fault? I listened...he wasn't singing any more duff notes than usual. Then it clicked. We had become connoisseurs of worship instead of participants in it...Then the truth came to us:

worship is not a spectator sport, it is not a product moulded by the taste of the consumer. It is all about God.

We needed to take drastic action. So we banned the band. For a couple of months the church services were totally different: nobody led worship – if someone wanted to sing they started a song. If not we would have silence. We agreed that if no one brought a sacrifice of praise we would spend the meeting in silence. At the beginning we virtually did! It was a very painful process. We were learning again not to rely on the music. After a while we began to have some very sweet times of worship. We all began to bring our prayers, our readings, our prophecies, our thanksgiving, our praise and our songs…The excitement came back. We were once again meeting with God. With all the comforts stripped away people worshipped from the heart.

When we had learned the lesson we brought the band back. It was at this point that Matt began to sing the song he had written out of this experience, 'The Heart of Worship – When The Music Fades.' The words express exactly what was going on.

> I'm coming back to the heart of worship
> And it's all about You Jesus.
> I'm sorry Lord for the thing I've made it
> When it's all about you, all about you Jesus.'[25]

Dan Lucani who was for many years a praise and worship leader in the Christian Contemporary Music Movement, until he became disillusioned shares his understanding of the 'true heart of worship.' He perceives that the phrase 'the heart of worship' originates from the truth that God looks at the inward heart of man. A truth the Lord shared with Samuel when he anointed David as king. However, he found that this phrase was used by those in the Christian Contemporary Music scene to justify any style or choice of music. He also came to see that the very meaning of the word 'worship' changed.

> It no longer refers to the biblical practice of bowing in reverence and humility before a holy God. The word itself has been expanded beyond this basic meaning to include all the forms used for worship, any style of music played by any musician, dancing, drama and art. It can mean the service itself and anything that occurs within it.[26]

He points out that contemporary music styles have a heavily syncopated beat, such as soft rock, smooth jazz, rap and pop/rock. 'Rock and roll is a musical style that was created for immoral purposes by immoral men and has always been used by the world to express its immoral attitudes in song. You have probably heard this before but it is worth repeating here. The name 'rock and roll' originated from a slang phrase for having sex. Rock music is the over-whelming preference of the sexually immoral, of wild parties, of the strip joints, of drunks and of drug abusers.'[27] His statement may be controversial to some and way off beam to others, who use this style of music in worship without any of the connections or inclinations he mentions. It can also be considered spot on by others.

Lucarni points out that in the Old Testament the Hebrew word translated as worship is *shacach*–to prostrate (especially in homage to God): to bow oneself down, to crouch, to fall down flat, to humbly beseech. In the New Testament the Greek word translated most commonly as worship is *proskuneo*, which means to kiss like a dog licking his master's hand: to prostrate oneself in homage. He concludes by saying: 'The true heart of worship is when the attitude of our heart is in complete submission to God. We have nothing to offer God except our total devotion and obedience.'[28]

He believes that a major problem with the contemporary notion of worship is that God wants to affirm us through worship and make us feel good about ourselves. He implies that at the heart of this style of worship is the 'feel good factor.' Whereas for him to achieve a good personal feeling is not part of biblical worship. It is not about raising hands and having a feeling of intimacy. 'Worship is about bowing down and feeling lowly. True worship is about producing a sense of the fear of the Lord. The true heart of worship is the heart that bows before God and submits to His Word – no more and no less.'[29] Lucarni's understanding of the heart of worship initially seems as if it soundly contradicts Soul Survivor's ethos. But, on closer examination, the two stances can be seen to be complimentary – where there is no desire to manipulate the ethos of the heart in worship.

## CONTEMPORARY WORSHIP MUSIC

Rob Redman informs us that 'Contemporary worship is identified with certain musical style such as – rock, pop, gospel, R & B and hip-hop. A song composed since 1970 can fit this style. Contemporary Worship Music did not evolve from any denominational culture. It has its roots in a commercial production culture – a network of songwriters, artists, producers, publishers and distributors. Their assumptions, beliefs and goals have shaped this genre of song since the 70s as well as the theological content and attitude towards worship.'[30]

He also points out that the background of this style of worship evolved from a personal expression of faith and worship as these songs were written in the first person singular – *something we clearly see in many contemporary songs* (italics mine) unlike many hymns that are statements about God. Also the songs were short and were to be sung repeatedly – again unlike hymns and gospel songs that develop over several verses. Brevity and simplicity are the hallmark of these songs and repetition allowed the worshipper to sing with emotion or from the heart.[31]

Redman says: 'there are four major producers of CWM – Maranatha Music, the Vineyard Music Group, Integrity Music and Worship Together. By the mid 80s Christian Contemporary Music and CWM were firmly established in at least some parts of the Evangelical Protestant world and in particular among independent charismatic churches. The newcomer among the big four is EMI Christian Music and its CWM label Worship Together. This began in the late 1990s for a new generation of younger worship leaders and songwriters from the United Kingdom such as Martin Smith, Matt Redman, Stuart Townsend, Noel Richards and Chris Tomlin. Large Christian gatherings such as Spring Harvest and Soul Survivor added momentum to this style of worship, that has been strongly influenced by the alternative rock sounds of bands like U2.'[32]

He also perceives that 'one Characteristic feature of Christian Contemporary Music is that this genre is generally artist orientated,while another is the songs are usually written for artists not congregations. They are meant for solo or ensemble performances not congregational singing and the artists perform a song in an personal style – although this doesn't always translate well when sung by a congregation. While there is concern that the business practice of the companies producing contemporary worship is turning this into a commercial product that can create a conflict of interest between God's values and human values, the Christian music industry is influential and largely successful in shaping this genre of worship.'[33]

## THE LYRICS OF CONTEMPORARY SONGS
Before sharing some observations about Soul Survivor songs, I would like to acknowledge Matt Redman's call and gifting as an outstanding contemporary song-writer and

worship leader. His integrity in seeking to express his love
for the Lord is transparent in his book 'The Unquenchable
Worshipper.' In this he describes how he felt as a young
teenager when the Lord touched his heart and he was
bursting to express his love for Him, but didn't know how. 'I
was desperate to somehow let this worship out.'[34] I shan't
tell the end of this story but it makes the important point that
Matt's repertoire of songs flows from his love for the Lord.
A main aim of this style of worship is to enable Christians
to express their love for the Lord. This is arguably Soul
Survivor's most distinctive contribution to worship. Also,
their contribution to the spiritual growth of many young
people is incalculable. The DVD 'In Spirit & Truth'–2006
shares the enormous debt of gratitude young people owe S.S.

Having looked at the ethos of the heart of worship in Soul
Survivor, I shall now look at the lyrics of Matt Redman's
and S. S. songs and compare these with Graham Kendrick's
songs and those of Spring Harvest. The Soul Survivor
songbook I look at is S. S. 4 – 2001. This has 55 songs by
Matt Redman and 145 by other artists. S. S. songbook 2006
has 12 songs by Matt Redman and 135 by other artists. In
S. S. 2006 there are no songs about justice, oppression and
the poor except for no: 7 & 30. Soul Survivor songbooks
contain songs by the artists who are involved at the festival,
and it is their lyrics I objectively aim to critique.

Looking through the S. S. 2001 songbook certain things
stood out that I had not previously noticed during sung
worship. The songs generally do not rhyme and are free
style prose so it would be difficult to remember or memorise
the majority of them. I observed that very few are based on
a passage of Scripture that unfolds as the song progresses,
although their lyrics might well be inspired by a Bible
passage. Nevertheless, there may well be around 12 well
known songs that will still be sung in years to come.

As I looked through the S. S. Songbook 2001 that has 200 songs of which 55 are Matt Redman's, in 70% – 140 songs, the focus of the songs was not the Lord – but the believer. Out of 55 Matt Redman songs 75% focused on the believer. While the songs allude to or mention God and Christ they are *about* the believer and how he/she feels. Yet there is an obvious intimacy expressed in them as the writer is either singing to the Lord in the context of his relationship with Him, or asking the Lord to do things for him/her. While the songs are addressed to God and Christ the believer can still be seen as being the subject.

The lyrics of the majority of these songs didn't strike me as aesthetically worshipful on their own – although I am aware this may be a subjective perception. When I mentioned this to my wife she pointed out it is the music that makes them worshipful. If a significant number of this genre of songs are to be around in a few years time, would it help if the artists widened their style of composition? To what extent would it make them more memorable if more of the lyrics rhymed? Would it be helpful to base a song on a passage of scripture that unfolds the truths it contains as the song progresses? Would it add to their longevity to ensure that God and Christ are the object and subject of their lyrics?

In fairness to Soul Survivor I looked through the Graham Kendrick collection of 150 songs published in 2000. I also found the majority of his songs do not rhyme, and many of the lyrics also did not strike me as worshipful on their own. They too would have to be accompanied by music. However, there are around 20 well known hymns/songs spanning the last 25 years or so that struck me as being memorable and will probably still be around in another 25 years. What was transparently clear about Graham's songs/hymns was that almost all of them focus on Jesus – and not on the believer in the way Soul Survivor does.

Also, in fairness to Soul Survivor I looked through the
Spring Harvest songbook 2006–7 that contains 120 songs
of which 75 are new. This included 7 G. Kendrick songs, 7
M. Redman songs and 7 by Tim Hughes. The analysis of this
S. H. collection was very similar to that of S. S. and G. K.
The songs are free style prose composition and only a
handful rhyme. Although the index gives just over 3 pages
of Scripture references to the songs I did not recognise many
biblical references in them. Presumably these Scripture
passages have inspired the writers, but the lyrics of their
songs do not draw out their biblical truth. Only a handful of
songs struck me as memorable and they were the S. S. songs.
On their own the lyrics of the S. H songs also did not strike
me as intrinsically worshipful. They like S. S songs and
G. K. songs would also need music to add this dimension.
Just over 50% of the songs were about God or Jesus: 20%
were about 'me' – although this genre of song is different
from the S. S. songs that focus on the individual: just over
10% were about us as believers and just under 10% were
about others – for instance about justice.

Nick Page in his provocative title 'And Now Let's Move
Into A Time Of Nonsense' – considers that contemporary
songs are failing the church. He says: 'They often don't
scan very well, they frequently attempt rhymes that you
could only call 'optimistic' – they're often little more than a
collection of Bible verses ripped out of context and shoe-
horned into a lyric.'[35] Matt Redman has some helpful things
to say about song-writing. He refers to what Jesus said in
Matt. 12: 34: 'out of the abundance of the heart the mouth
speaks' – (King James translation).

> It conjures up a great picture of having so much love
> in our hearts for God that we can hardly keep it in.
> That's the starting point with song-writing. Make
> sure it's not just some clever words put together
> with a nice tune. A meaningful song will always be
> the passionate expression of your heart towards God.

'Sometimes you hear a song and it's got a lot of heart but doesn't sound like it's been worked on at all. It is meaningful but doesn't feel like it's been finished and made ready for congregations to use...Other times you'll hear a song and it has lots of words, perfect rhymes and a singable tune yet not much heart...it's missing that inspiration factor. The best songs have both – a mixture of heartfelt inspiration that has been carefully crafted for congregational use.'[36]

Nick Page puts his finger on the style of contemporary song writing when he says: 'Today the predominant model for verse-writing is the pop song. Today's songs are written by people steeped in rock and roll and rock music traditions. Songs are not published as poems to be read but tunes to be played. This is a huge change. Pop brings with it its own views of the lyrics. In poetry what matters are the words – the metaphors, the images, the rhythm and the structures. In pop songs what matters is the melody, the hook, the beat...We don't publish the words of our worship songs as poetry collections today – because these poems are not worth reading.'[37] If the lyrics of these songs are compared to the Psalms, the model for intimacy in worshipping the Lord, the Psalms have a superior theological content. If these songs are also compared to well known hymns again many of their lyrics would equally not match their theological content. As you read through these hymns a theme evolves through the verses and you often sense that the writer has penned them from a profound experience of God and Christ – although on occasions I also sensed this was true of contemporary songs. There are in fact books written that share the stories behind the composition of well known hymns and these testify to the authors' spiritual experience that led to the inspiration to write them. (See 'An Annotated Anthology Of Hymns' – J. R. Watson Oxford University Press: also two books on preaching on hymns – F. Colquhoun – Mowbray).

The Rev Peter Moger, The National Worship Development Officer for The Church of England, offers his perspective about worship songs and hymns. 'Worship songs are markedly different from hymns and require different criteria of assessment. There are many varieties of song – Jeremy Begbie has isolated six distinct types – but central to them all is the conviction that worship has to do with a personal relationship between the worshipper and God. One might differentiate between hymns sung about God and songs addressed to God. This is sometimes a false distinction but it does highlight a major difference between the two.

Many worship songs lack substantial theological content. Arguably they make greater sense when placed within a worship context, but sometimes the words themselves could realistically be sung by anyone, regardless of their faith. Some texts make no mention of God while a large number are guilty of sentimentalism. To examine only the words of worship song, though, is to miss the point. They need to be put with their music and then sung by a congregation which longs to express itself through singing. The cerebral content assumes less of a priority in songs than in hymns. Nevertheless, it is a mistake to assume that any hymn or song may be reduced to its words.

> Much renewal music transmits a message of joy without tears, glory without suffering, resurrection without crucifixion. Human weakness is seldom acknowledged, sin and suffering are often dismissed. Church music must avoid the temptation to stay with the cosy and familiar – and if it is to be prophetic, it must disturb as well as console. Good church music will display theological integrity and musical quality. Important too, is the integrity of the act of worship as a whole – for church music is only one amongst many vehicles for the worship of God's people.'[38]

While all contemporary songs-writers would undoubtedly claim the inspiration of their songs comes from Scripture, the actual theological content – the amount of biblical truth they actually contain is often not very high. John 4: 23-24 highlights the importance Jesus placed on worshipping God in spirit and truth.

> But the hour is coming and now is, when true worshippers will worship the Father in spirit and truth, for such the Father seeks to worship him. God is spirit and those who worship him must worship in spirit and truth.

D. Carson reminds us that 'God is spirit' means God is divine, invisible and unknowable unless he chooses to reveal himself – but these are elements of God's gracious self-disclosure in His Son. In and through Jesus he may be known as truly as is possible. 'The worshippers whom God seeks worship Him out of the fullness of the supernatural life they enjoy ('in spirit') and on the basis of God's incarnate Self-Expression – Christ Jesus himself, through whom God's person and will are finally and ultimately disclosed ('in truth').'[39] Commentators also point out that worship of the Father can only take place in and through Jesus. C. K. Barrett echoes this: 'True worship takes place in and through him....It is here that the other sense of 'spirit' makes itself felt, for the Spirit, the Paraclete, brings home to men the truth revealed in Jesus (14: 24, 16: 14).'[40]

L. Morris has this to say about John 4: 23-24: 'Notice the word 'must'– Jesus is not speaking of merely a desirable element in worship. He is speaking of something that is absolutely necessary...People cannot dictate the 'how' or the 'where' of worship. They must come only in the way that the Spirit of God opens for them.'[41] R. E. Brown draws our attention in these verses to worshipping the Father in the Spirit. 'God can only be worshipped as Father by those who possess the Spirit that makes them God's children...verse 24

couples Spirit and truth. In 17: 7-9 we shall hear that the
truth is an agent of consecration and sanctification, and
thus truth also enables man to worship God properly. The
Johannine themes are closely intertwined: Jesus is the truth
(14: 6) in the sense that he reveals God's truth to men (8: 45,
18: 37): the Spirit is the Spirit of Jesus and is the Spirit of
truth (14: 17, 15: 26) who is to guide men into truth. Thus it
would be foolish to ask what the Spirit contributes to
worship as distinct from what truth contributes.'[42] We cannot
speak too strongly about the centrality of truth in worship –
because the depth and substance of a Service is to a large
extent determined by the biblical content of its component
parts. The centrality of the truth is also of great importance –
because those who long to deepen their worship, may find
they can begin to do this by ensuring all the component parts
of a Service, are immersed in and overflowing with biblical
truth–undergirded by prayer and anointed by the Holy Spirit.

J.M. Boice draws our attention to three aspects of the truth.
He reminds us of the need to approach God truthfully and
honestly – as opposed to 'those who honour me with their
lips, but their heart is far from me' – Matt. 15: 8-9. A
reminder that what we bring to worship the Lord on Sunday
is what we have been during the week – and if that has not
been right we must come and be truthful about it. He also
emphasises that we must worship on the basis of biblical
revelation. If we are to worship in truth as God commands,
we must do so in accordance with the principles of Scripture.
He also brings us to the essence of worship – for to approach
God in truth means we must approach Christocentrically.[43]

Christians know that Jesus is the one *by* whom and *in*
whom and *through* whom and *with* whom we are able to
approach God in our worship. We do not come to worship
God through the excellence of our love no matter how
wonderful it is. We do not come through our outstanding
style of worship. We come through Christ because he is the

way to the Father and the truth about Him. These truths are particularly important, because on the one hand some Christians may feel their love for the Lord is really powerful and strong and want to express this in sung worship. Whereas other Christians will feel their love for the Lord is inconsistent and nowhere as impressive. For them their confidence in worshipping the Lord lies not in their love, but in the fact Christ is the one who has made it possible to come and worship. Of course those whose love for the Lord is strong still need to hold onto the truth, that they too come to worship through Christ. Therefore, those who lead sung worship would do well to remember that songs that speak about the believer's love for the Lord may be difficult for some to join in. In the first part of a Service an emphasis on reassuring believers of God's acceptance and Christ's forgiveness and restoration, can give them confidence and help them respond in gratitude and love to the Lord in sung worship.

As we reflect on the necessity of truth in worship, what we sing also has to be rooted in and reflect the truth about God, Christ and ourselves. As ransomed children of God we come to sing about the truths of the Gospel and the truths that reflect who God is, who Christ is and who the Spirit is. So in the context of contemporary worship care should be taken to ensure that what we sing about is the truth contained in Scripture. This enables us to be objective about the emotional content and subjective feelings expressed in our worship songs. It allows us to ask: 'what truths does this song contain that the lyrics are expressing?' Asking such questions also helps us to ensure that what we sing is a response to biblical truth and has theological integrity. J. M. Boice shares his concern about the place of feelings in worship:

It may be the case, and often is, that the emotions are stirred in real worship. At times tears fill the eyes or joy floods the heart. But, unfortunately, it is possible for these things to happen and still no worship to be there. It is possible to be moved by a song or by preaching and yet not come to a genuine awareness of God and a fuller praise of his ways and nature.[44]

## TRADITIONAL HYMNS

In the local parish church in the Communion Service they use the hymnbook,'Common Praise.' This primarily contains traditional hymns along with some contemporary ones. One of the things I have valued about these hymns is that the Lord has often spoken to me through them. This is not surprising as they contain a high level of doctrine and is one of the reasons they were written. I also value them as they remind me of the Christians I worshipped with many years ago as a youngster. Moreover many of these hymns have lovely harmonies and tunes. It is striking to read about the care taken in the composition of hymns that 'An Annotated Anthology Of Hymns' speaks about although the language is a bit dated:

> A hymn must have a beginning, middle and end. There should be a manifest gradation in the thoughts and their mutual dependence should be so perceptible that they could not be transposed without injuring the unity of the piece: every line carrying forward the connection and every verse adding a well proportioned *part* to a symmetrical *piece*.[45] (*italics are mine*).

It is no surprise to learn that Isaac Watts who wrote over 400 hymns was an educated man and a prolific author who wrote sixty books and who had studied several languages.[46] It is also not surprising to learn that C. Wesley's hymns:

...are controlled by a craftsmanship which came from his classical education and by a natural poetic skill. Again and again a line or a verse of his hymns seems to be exactly right, to say what it wants to say with a richness of vocabulary and an economy of diction – and instantly recognisable as the work of a master.[47]

It is striking that traditional hymns are not comparatively old. Isaac Watts the most famous early father of English hymns had his work published in the 18th century. His hymns include: 'O God, Our Help In Ages Past,' 'When I Survey The Wondrous Cross' and 'Joy To The World.' His hymns were written to tie in with the meanings of his sermons and he believed they had to be more than just the repetition of Scripture – and authentic Christian worship had to include original personal expressions of faith. It is Watts more than any other man who established the model for hymns we sing today. Crucially he saw his task as writing for ordinary people. It is of interest to note that by the end of the 19th century there were around 400,000 hymns in use and it is reckoned that out of these there are only about 200 really fine hymns.[48] A salutary lesson for today's song-writers. Also, hymns originally were written as poetry to be read. The story goes that Isaac Watts complained to his father about the Psalms that were sung in church to which   he duly replied: 'Then write something better' – which is what he did.[49]

Charles and John Wesley, Anglican priests and hymn-writers whose origins were in the high church tradition, had a sacramental background rooted in the 'Book of Common Prayer.' They received Communion 'more often than not, twice a week' and Charles wrote many Eucharistic hymns that were published in 1745 as 'Hymns on the Lord's Supper.' This hymnbook was the 'most circulated and continuously used of all Methodist hymnbooks.' Yet Charles and John Wesley had no conflict between their Evangelical faith and the sacramental reality of Christian experience.[50] It is significant that the formative influence of these prolific hymn writers was Scripture and the Book of Common Prayer. John said: 'I believe there is no liturgy in the world, either in ancient or modern language, which breathes more of a solid, scriptural, rational Piety, than the Common Prayer of the Church of England.'[51]

C. Cocksworth in 'Evangelical Eucharistic Thought In The 20th Century' – draws our attention to the intimacy and union with Christ the believer can experience in the Communion Service John Wesley advocated. His theology was driven by a yearning for both the love of God and the loving of God that is clearly seen in the Eucharist. 'This is seen in the twin emphases of his theological practice: the presentation of the Gospel and the call to holiness, that are intrinsically located in the Eucharist. Wesley's passionate belief was that the Eucharist is a context – in fact, a peculiarly appropriate context – in which this could happen.

> Some, believe, and find Him here:
> Believe, and feel he died for you.

He also points out that Wesley's defence of the means of grace concentrated on the Lord's Supper, concerning a particular controversy he was involved in. The hymn he quotes to justify his understanding of grace explains his appeal to Scripture and his experience – and also affirms that intimacy with Christ is intrinsically located in the Service of Holy Communion that also embraces the Gospel.

> Why did my dying Lord ordain
> This dear memorial of His Love?
> Might we not all by faith obtain,
> By faith the mountain of sin remove,
> Enjoy the sense of sins forgiven,
> And holiness, the taste of heaven?
> It seem'd to my Redeemer good
> That faith should here His coming wait.

The prayer, the fast, the word conveys,
When mixed with faith, the life to me:
In all the channels of thy grace
I still have fellowship with Thee:
But chiefly there my soul is fed
With fullness of immortal bread.
Communion closer far I feel,
And deeper drink the atoning blood.'[52]

The desire for intimacy with the Lord that the Communion Service offers is not an end in itself. It brings with it the call to holiness – a sign of our desire of union with Christ. It is also striking to note the evangelistic emphasis the Wesleys placed on the Eucharist. Considering the outstanding results of their preaching ministries, it is surprising Evangelicals in the Church of England only have Communion once a month at their main Service.

## IT'S ALL ABOUT ME JESUS

One aspect of contemporary sung worship is the focus on intimacy with the Lord. As I read the lyrics because the believer is often the central focus, it struck me this genre of songs may reflect the adolescent phase of being in love with the feeling of love. Are these songs expressing more of a 'spiritual adolescence' because they focus on the believers' feelings so much? David Stancliffe, the Bishop of Salisbury, a member of the Church of England Liturgical Commission, echoes a similar concern.

At the moment too many of the texts of worship songs are theologically unadventurous or even worse. They can give the impression of concentrating on the worshipper's feelings and emotions rather than on celebrating what God has done for us and inviting a response. Greater experience of co-operation between songwriters, liturgists and theologians will be important if we are to create the kind of liturgy in which people can both articulate their usual patterns of worship, and also find a way in which the beliefs held in the authorised liturgy of the Church of England can actually be made to work in a variety of different contexts.[53]

N. Page also questions the lyrics of contemporary songs when he says: 'Our worship songs are more about creating feelings than helping understanding. Songs talk less and less about the attributes of God, or the work of Jesus and more about – well me. You cannot read a modern collection of worship songs without noticing the prominent use of 'I' or 'me.' In one collection I estimated that over half the songs were to do with the individual and his relationship with God. Obviously this is not wrong in itself: the same mode of expression can be found in many Psalms. But when so many songs talk about 'I' and when such phrases such as 'I want' or 'make me' or 'give me' arrive in such numbers, it is difficult to escape the feeling that I should only be interested in God for how He makes me feel.'[54]

Yet the desire for intimacy is a legitimate one as Jesus himself spoke of the closeness between himself and the Father his followers could expect to enjoy. But it is important to be aware that intimacy is not the sole aim of worship. It is also an integral part of fellowship with God and Christ in our lives. We see evidence of this on the Day of Pentecost. Once the excitement of receiving the Spirit and seeing around 3,000 converted had taken place, the disciples would have been aware of something unprecedented. After the crowd dispersed, it dawned on them that receiving the Holy Spirit meant that Christ and the Father were now with them in their hearts. The Holy Spirit brought them into an intimacy with Christ and the Father. This is the interpretation of baptism in the Holy Spirit at Pentecost. A fulfillment of what Jesus himself promised in John 14: 18, 20:

> I will not leave you desolate: I will come to you. In
> that day you will know that I am in my Father, and
> you in me and I in you.

Moreover Jesus also alludes to this intimacy again in John
14: 23:

> If a man loves me he will keep my word and my
> Father will love him and we will come to him and
> make our home with him.

This indicates that there should be no dichotomy between
seeking intimacy during corporate worship and intimacy
with Christ and the Father in our lives.

As a young teenage Christian and young adult, I found
great contentment and wholeness having the presence and
friendship of Christ in my heart. In those days I didn't refer
to this as intimacy but that is exactly what it was. Equally, in
later years I also experienced this closeness with God as
Father. I wrote a few lines twenty-five years ago to describe
this intimacy.

> I love you – though you are unseen
> Yet you dwell inside my being.
> Exactly what does my love mean
> to you – that you are receiving?
>
> You have become the intimacy
> My soul has constantly yearned for.
> Through all my life's changes I see
> You're more to me than I had before.

One of the features of contemporary songs is that they
often sing to 'Him' or 'You.' Although the believer knows
this refers either to Christ or God is there any reason why the
name Lord, Jesus or God is not used instead? Contemporary
songs by various writers also focus on the individual singing
to the Lord or receiving from him. It would reinforce being
part of the body of Christ if the 'I' was substituted by 'we.'

Is contemporary worship characterised by loud music in danger of inadvertently becoming an idol that we worship? The Old Testament prophets such as Isaiah declared that God's people had turned wood and stone into idols and incorporated them into their worship – Isa. 44: 13-17. There is a danger of giving the glory of God to things in our worship other than God – and this is a temptation we should be aware of. Loud music in sung worship also runs the risk of making worshippers feel they are spectators at a Christian rock concert rather than taking part in worship. Paul Oakley echoes this: 'Building a style of worship meeting that relies heavily on the band and the worship leader up front to lead us can, if we are not careful, bring about a spectator mentality.'[55]

One of the expectations people may have after attending Christian holidays or conferences, is that they return with a desire for their church to have the same celebratory style of worship. Having a band replicating the worship of 'Soul Survivor' or 'New Wine' seems straightforward enough, if you have able musicians and the minister is for this. What musicians tend to overlook is they can lead sung worship as if there are 3000+ people present – when in reality it can be between 100–300. It is clear that you do not play at the same volume for this number of people as you do for ten times that many. I am aware that loud music is not as worshipful to everyone and can have the opposite effect that is intended. While there is a biblical precedence to make a joyful noise to the Lord does this have to be accompanied by music that is unnecessarily loud? Making a joyful noise to the Lord with loud music can be seen to be justifiable and a matter of preference – but is there any reason why it isn't set at a level that is comfortable for everyone? One way to arrive at the right level is to ensure the congregational singing is noticeably louder than the band. This allows everyone to hear the lovely harmonies and melodies coming from the congregation as they express their worship to the Lord. Of course this are times when it is appropriate for the music to be louder to accentuate celebration, joy and victory.

Although they are obvious questions it seems reasonable that musicians should consider – 'In what ways does loud music make the sung worship more worshipful? And is sung worship more worshipful with overtly loud music – or is it just a matter of preference and style? To what extent does loud music deflect attention away from the Lord and onto the musicians and the music?' Having experienced sung worship where the band didn't play loudly it was clear that the beautiful harmonies and melodies of the congregation could be heard above the music. Darlene Szschech offers her outlook on music and worship.

> True worship is not about the songs being sung: it is not about the size of the band: it is not about the size of the choir. Although music is a wonderful expression of worship, it is not in itself the essence of it. The core of worship is when one's heart and soul and all that is within, adores and connects with the Spirit of God. In fact regardless of how magnificent the musical moments are, unless one's heart is fully engaged in the worship being expressed – it is still only music. The song of a pure heart that is yearning for more of God and less of oneself, is the music that holds the key to so many victories and delights the heart of our King.[56]

There is a clear distinction between musicians performing and leading God's people in worship. To counteract the temptation to perform one of the principles I have always embraced as a preacher, is to pray that the Lord would point people to himself through me. This ensures my motivation and manner when ministering in public is right and does not draw attention to myself. This principle is of primary importance when a band of musicians leads the sung worship. Such issues as motivation, the style of the worship, the loudness of the music and how it is led, should be guided by the principle of 'pointing people to the Lord.' The temptation to perform may also lead to 'hyping-up' the worship that can be seen as the 'main event.' This can lead to pressure to manipulate peoples' emotions and as a result can lack integrity in worship. The temptation to hype can involve the repetition of songs that isn't always appropriate. Tim Hughes shares an example of Mike Pilavachi writing a letter to the worship leaders at his church about this and he shares part of what he wrote.

> Do not only prepare your choice of songs but also how you will lead them. Never repeat a song for no reason. We are singing songs for too long at the moment. It is boring and pointless. If you are going to repeat a song then think what you meant to emphasise the second time. You can change the emphasis by changing the instrumentation. To repeat a song with the same musical backing, tempo and vocal emphasis is just laziness. Don't do it any more.

Tim comments that being Greek Mike is prone to making the point somewhat strongly but adds that he is right.[57]

From the lyrics of the S. S. songs one conclusion to objectively come to is that they are essentially: 'all about me Jesus.' This is not a cynical nor a derogatory comment. Neither is it intended to be controversial as it is an accurate observation. Pete Ward a lecturer at King's College, London, and author of 'Selling Worship – How What We Sing Has Changed The Church,' comes to the same conclusion.

> Matt Redman is clear in 'When The Music Fades' that the heart of worship is all about you Jesus. This is a crucial insight but it could be observed that very few songs are really all about Jesus. In fact many of the songs including 'When The Music Fades' are not

really all about Jesus at all: rather they are all about the worshipper and their experiences in worship. In other words the songs leave themselves open to the criticism that they have replaced the content of the Christian gospel with human experience. Instead of worshipping Jesus they give the impression that we are worshipping worship. In other words it could be said that this trend in contemporary worship is in danger of being accused of a kind of idolatry.[58]
Nevertheless, it is appropriate to affirm that the genre of S. S. worship has enabled God's people – especially young people to express their love for the Lord.

As the focus of a large number of contemporary songs is the believer, the biblical truth they contain about God and Christ can be low. To what extent does this limit the content of sung worship? As a result in what ways does it also restrict our experience of God and Christ in worship too? The Rev. Dr. Christopher Cocksworth, the Principal of Ridley Hall in Cambridge, and a member of the Liturgical Commission of the Church of England, echoes his concern about contemporary and traditional worship.

I grieve the two (false) choices that seem to be on offer in so many places I visit: 'traditional churches' with a lifeless form of liturgical worship or 'modern Evangelical' churches with a reductionist, liturgy-less form of worship.

(Soul Survivor and contemporary worship invariably fits the latter description. He believes that authentic Catholic-Evangelical worship is necessarily charismatic – and his comprehensive vision of worship is wide-ranging in its inclusiveness, in comparison to the diet of contemporary worship.)

> ...Evangelical worship refuses to reduce these intensive moments of worship to the modes of exaltation and adoration – what might be called the 'sacrifice of praise'– still less to particular feelings of worship experienced by the emotions of the spirit in the giving of thanks and praise. Evangelical worship, worship according to the Gospel is heard and seen, celebrated and received, expressed, embodied and enacted: the reading and preaching of scripture, the gathering, praying, singing and dismissal of the people...More specifically Catholic-Evangelical worship in the Spirit will have the capacities to hold together that which the flawed history of Christian worship and spirituality has forced apart: word and sacrament, prophetic and mystical, personal and communal, simple and ceremonial, ordered and spontaneous, exaltation and edification.[59]

Robin Parry's book 'Worshipping Trinity' – 2005 has an arresting sub-title: 'Coming back to the heart of worship.' Only for him the heart of worship is Trinitarian and all about God the Father, the Son and the Holy Spirit. In his first chapter he shares how being a mild mannered charismatic he pondered just how Trinitarian contemporary charismatic worship really is. He was prompted to think about this as one Sunday morning after returning home from worship, he was disturbed because neither the Father nor the Spirit had received even as much as a passing glance.

> The leader opened the meeting with a call to worship: 'We've come together this morning to meet with Jesus.' We then proceeded to sing numerous songs all directed to Jesus or 'You Lord' who was also Jesus. There were numerous prayers all directed to Jesus. The sermon waxed eloquent about Jesus, but his Father and the Spirit didn't get a look in.

When he went home he randomly selected one of the best
selling worship music CDs over the last few years and
looked at the contents of these songs. Reading the lyrics was
an eye-opener for him as there was no mention of either God
the Father or the Holy Spirit. All the songs were addressed
either to Jesus or to an anonymous god or lord. There was no
mention of the incarnation of Jesus, the ministry of Jesus, the
resurrection or the ascension. Only one song mentioned the
cross. But there was a great balance on intimacy.[60]

 Parry also perceives the danger of such minimalist songs
is that 'if they become dominant, we gradually lose sight
of the biblical Christ and replace him with – 'Jesus-my-
personal-therapist' or 'Jesus-my-girlfriend.''These are vague
characters who give worshippers warm fuzzy feelings of
acceptance, but I think one has to seriously ask whether such
Christs are the real Christ at all. If such songs dominate
worship meetings one has to ask at what point worship
ceases to be *Christian* worship and degenerates into some
mutant offering?'[61]

He also observes it would be true to say that contemporary
Christian worship of Jesus is 'to the glory of God the Father
– and it is true that whenever Jesus is present the Father is
present too, but this is not an excuse for the neglect of the
Father and the Spirit. There are a couple of fairly recent
songs that proclaim – 'it's all about you Jesus' and in a sense
this is true and they are worshipful.

> However, taken in a fairly straightforward sense the
> claim is simply  false. *It is not all about Jesus*. It is
> all about God – Father, Son  and Holy  Spirit. My
> concern about songs like that is that the ordinary
> person in the congregation, probably doesn't interpret
> the song in a suitably qualified way and simply runs
> with  the  straightforward  (false)  meaning, perhaps
> undermining  little  by  little,  the  place  of  the  Father

and Spirit in their own spirituality. I want to suggest that the worship of Jesus is central to Christianity, and that it is honouring to both Father and Spirit, but that it must not move towards an exclusive focus on worshipping Jesus that denies the reality of the Trinity by pushing the Father and the Spirit to the margins. Trinitarian spirituality requires a balance that some are in danger of losing.'[62]

## AN APPRAISAL OF CHARISMATIC WORSHIP
James Steven in 'Worship In The Spirit – Charismatic Worship In The Church Of England,' carried out a study of worship in six charismatic churches over a 2 year period between 1993-1994. Three churches were Evangelical, one was Anglo-Catholic, another was modern Catholic and the other was in an urban priority area. His research provides some important insights that merit serious consideration.

Steven perceives the cultural backdrop to charismatic worship is the popular culture that evolved from the 1960s counter-culture. This emphasised individual participation, expressiveness, impatience with formality and institutional life. The romantic songs of pop culture are seen as a type of the intimate style of songs in charismatic worship. A comparison is made with the disco culture that moves from songs with an upbeat dance rhythm to slower songs of romantic intimacy. He says:

> Traditional liturgies and symbols lose the scale and complexity needed to engage congregations with society, tradition and history.Spirituality is redefined: Christians identify their deepest religious experiences 'not with public ritual and worship, but with private, personal experiences of intimacy and relationship' – and so live with a model of the sacred that is based on intimacy, not liturgy. The consequence of this intimisation is the Church's loss of the sense of the

public nature of worship: 'the journey into intimate community is a journey out of the public world,' with the result that the Church is unable to transform the public sphere.[63]

He perceives that liturgy is more readily judged according to its therapeutic capacity to meet the needs of the individual rather than its ability to mediate ecclesiological significance. Worshippers now 'look for the holy to reveal itself not in the awe inspiring rite of Baptism and Eucharist, but in the awesome precincts of the self.'[64] Sobering words that challenge us to think about the identity of the Church as a Christian community. Is our worship engaging with the reality of our lives and the world, or are we creating a community that is inadvertently inward looking?

Steven noted that charismatic worship tends to focus on the dominant metaphor of Christ the Lord as the ascended, glorified, majestic King so that his divinity is powerfully celebrated. 'There is however a dilemma posed by this concentration upon the divine majestic Christ, namely the way that it obscures his humanity...in charismatic hymnody the exalted Christ has almost completely overshadowed the gospel accounts of Jesus of Nazareth...Instead of singing to a Jesus who in his humanity faced temptation, conflict and suffering – we sing to a triumphant Christ who in his majesty and power defeats the powers of evil.'[65]

He astutely observes that another important omission is any reference to Christ as our great high priest and his continuing priesthood in his risen humanity in the heavenly sanctuary. Instead Christ is located in the past in his atoning death on the cross.

The result of this was an experience of worship that had its entire center of gravity located with the worshippers, who invite the Spirit to join them in

their worship – in contrast to worship that is offered
with its center of gravity located *in*, *with* and *through*
the priestly Christ in his offering to the Father.
The invitation that remained unarticulated in sung
worship was Christ's invitation to join him in his life
of worship. An invitation identified by Christopher
Cocksworth as a central theme of early apostolic
witness in the New Testament. 'Christ invites us into
the redeemed humanity which he bears, the new
creation which he brings to birth and the holy city
which he has entered. The invitation is to accompany
him into the glory of God.[66]

We have already noted many of the lyrics of contemporary
songs tend to focus on the believer as the subject. One
unspoken inference is that Christians *in* and *of* themselves
can offer their worship to God. This implies their worship
has intrinsic value *in* and *of* itself. This can lead to a wrong
approach and wrong attitudes in worship – and the inherent
danger is it bypasses the truth – that it is only *in* and *through*
Christ that we have *access to the Father*. And it is only in
and through Christ our great high priest we can *offer*
*acceptable worship to God*. This is the starting point of our
worship, rather than the feelings of the believers, or the
worship they come to offer.

Similarly, Steven identifies that one of the features of
charismatic worship is its estrangement from a dynamic
relationship with Christ's offering of worship – in the way
that it draws attention to itself. Song lyrics tend to celebrate
the act of worship itself as much as the object of worship.
He points out that estranged from a dynamic relationship
to Christ's worship, the worshipping assembly believing
itself to be the only subject of true worship, appears to have
fallen into the temptation of gazing upon itself as it worships
'in the Spirit.' He quotes Tom Torrance who says:

> If there is no consciousness of our offering of worship being in, with and through Christ, then we are inevitably thrown back upon ourselves to offer worship to the Father: worship of our own devising, although it may be worship for the sake of Christ, motivated by him.[67]

This highlights that the theological content of our songs is important and begs the question: how worshipful to God are songs that have the believer as their object and primary focus? This also has implications for our identity as a Christian community and raises the issue of how we are being shaped by what we sing. Moreover, if we cannot theologically discern the content of contemporary songs – we may well be think our worship has reached a pinnacle of excellence and 'really rocks' – when it doesn't.

In his research Steven mentions what is commonly referred to as a 'time of worship.' 'Within such an environment there was no affirmation of the goal of worship being participation with Christ in the worship of the heavenly sanctuary, of which the letter to the Hebrews describes Christ as the leader (Heb. 8:2). This lack of reference to the transcendent and eschatological reality of heavenly worship becomes evident when charismatic songs are compared with the hymns of Charles Wesley. This is particularly marked in Wesley's hymns for the Ascension and Eucharist, which draws worshippers into the transcendent and eschatological reality of worship around the throne of God. In the presence of the wounded and interceding Priest and the company of the saints. For the Wesleys this vision of heavenly worship was the goal of all earthly worship. Another indicator of this impoverished lack of participation in heavenly worship, was the lack of genuinely ecstatic language in the songs. The Wesleys' hymns at their most ecstatic celebrate a movement beyond ourselves and into the unfathomable depths of the life of God, where we are 'lost in wonder, love and praise.'[68]

What may be termed the high point in a time of sung worship, is seen with the believer being absorbed in an intimate encounter with the Lord who comes among us by His Spirit – as opposed to being drawn by the same Spirit through Christ into the life of heavenly worship. 'Another aspect of the climax of the time of worship, that betrayed its disconnection with the eschatological goal of worship in Christ, was the individualism of its romantic intimacy. This nullifies the corporate consciousness of the charismatic assembly turning the body of Christ into a single 'I' in its communion with God. This is an obvious casualty of the pervasive influences of the two cultural trends of the intimacy and subjectivity of social reality...In contrast Charles Wesley's hymns depict the goal of Christian worship as an essentially corporate activity, standing with the redeemed community before the throne of God...Because worship for the Wesleys was offered through, in and with the ascended High Priest, their hymns avoid the individualism of the charismatic vision of communion with God.'[69]

From his research on six charismatic churches Steven noted that while the songs celebrated Christian joy, victory and confidence they did not embrace other areas of the believer's life – such as the cost of discipleship, or suffering and patient endurance in the face of opposition and lament for human sinfulness. He points out that Jeremy Begbie in his study of charismatic songs observed this same tendency. This is not surprising as in this genre of worship the humanity of Christ is overshadowed by his exalted divine glory. This serious defect in the church's worship is starkly captured by Tom Torrance's criticism:

> A mutilated humanity in Christ could not
> but result in a mutilated worship of God.

Consequently, because of this the Christian theme of hope in the face of suffering has been lost and the expression of human sinfulness has also been weakened.

This is reflected in the tendency of the 'heart' to be conceived romantically in charismatic hymnody, rather than the more biblical view of the heart as a moral center – which in Anglican tradition is given liturgical expression in Cranmer's Collect forPurity.[70]

In my experience the confession as a component part of contemporary worship tends to be a brief informal act that lacks meaningful Scriptural content – and as a result it is over very quickly. If worshippers have sinned in a way that troubles them and are feeling condemned, guilty or unworthy – it is unlikely that a brief diluted confession, robbed of the potency of Christ's forgiveness can bring his absolution. It is the responsibility of the person who is leading this part of worship, to ensure that the content is biblically substantial.

Tom Smail echoes a similar concern when in the 90s he spoke about the failure of charismatics to find a central and regular place in their worship, for the confession of sins and deep repentance, that God's free forgiveness evokes from us and creates in us. 'It is often remarked that every great renewal in the Spirit begins when he convicts Christ's people of their sins and leads them to repentance (John 16: 8-11). This has not so far been characteristic of the charismatic renewal, and the lack of it explains the impression of superficiality and even unreality, that the renewal and its worship can sometimes convey.'[71]

At the same time Smail shares that the beginning of charismatic renewal in the 70s was marked by a new release of praise, intimacy, freedom and a sense of the immediacy of God. The distinctive feature of charismatic worship was seen as the corporate and spontaneous singing in tongues often called 'singing in the Spirit.' 'Those of us who have actually participated in charismatic renewal worship, especially in its early days and our own early days in it, can bear witness that we have been carried not into some vague mystic ecstasies without Christian content, but into the kind of worship of the Ancient of Days and of the Lamb, who is in the midst of his throne that the book of Revelation describes. This has added to our corporate worship of God, a dimension of immediacy, directness, depth, freedom and joy to an extent that we did not know.'[72]

He also highlights the shortcomings of charismatic renewal that may well be a prophetic warning to those who are involved in contemporary and charismatic worship.

> Nevertheless, while we have every reason to speak with great gratitude of charismatic worship, we have at the same time to recognise that at the moment all is not well with it. Often in the seminars out of which this book emerged (1993) we heard ministers and other leaders who had been deeply involved in renewal and its worship over long periods, expressing perplexity and dismay that somehow or other the glory had departed from it: that the high praises of God had degenerated into endless repetitive chorus singing that was in danger of becoming a bore and a burden rather than a release and a joy: that the celebration of the saving acts of God has been replaced by pious self-indulgence in religious sentiment for its own sake: that people were sometimes being worked up or manipulated into a strained and artificial worship, that concealed God's absence mare than it responded to his presence.[73]

## TRANSFORMING WORSHIP

When Isaiah encountered God (Isa. ch. 6) the Lord didn't reveal himself in all His holiness and glory to give him a feeling of intimacy. He came to cleanse and commission him. Through worship he had a new vision of God and a renewed vision to serve. Matt Redman perceives that he was never the same again after this vision. 'Isaiah is broken, stunned and shaken in the presence of God. But this brokenness is not a destructive thing: God is stripping him apart in order to put him back as a stronger, purer worshipper – a worshipper whose heart cry is: 'Here am I Lord send me.' Of course there is a time to be joyful in worship, content and even comfortable. But there are times when God will make us distinctly uncomfortable. He puts us under the spotlight of His holiness where we begin to search our hearts more closely.'[74] Psalm 95 reminds us that as we progress from praising the Lord to worshipping Him we are exhorted to 'hearken to his voice.' For Isaiah this meant a response of obedient faith and a renewed call to serve the Lord. Intimate though his encounter with God was it was not an end in itself. His glimpse of heavenly worship transformed him and his ministry.

When Paul was writing to the Christians at Corinth he was addressing a charismatic church that used spiritual gifts in their worship. Although this caused problems it is instructive to note early on in 2 Corinthians 3: 18, that he refers to what we may call a truly 'charismatic phenomenon' when he says: 'And we all with unveiled face beholding the glory of the Lord are being changed from one degree of glory into another.' It is clear as you read this letter that this was not the case in this church. Nevertheless, Paul raises the possibility of spiritual transformation using Moses as an example of someone who used to stand in the presence of the Lord. Matt Redman perceives: 'Moses was ushered into an incredible level of revelation, so deep into the heart of God's glory that his face is actually shining. So radiant in fact that the people were afraid to look at him...That passage gives us insight into two things: the deep revelation of God and the change it brings to those who experience it. And the greater the revelation the greater the transformation.'[75] If we see the ultimate aim of worship as the Lord coming among us and revealing his glory, the pinnacle of our worship is not intimacy – but to be immersed in the overwhelming glory of the presence of the Lord: and to be transformed into the likeness of Christ – so that our faces and personalities radiate his glory.

## THE SONG OF THE LORD

Tamara Winslow shares one aspect of worship the Lord taught her. She calls this learning to 'sing the song of the Lord.' This changed her life and she can trace its roots back to when she was between eight and eleven years old and was due to sing on Easter Sunday – 'Were You There?' That morning while preparing to sing the reality of the words pierced her heart, and she became acutely aware of the conditions of the hearts of many people who would attend the service, and their need to know Jesus in a way they have never known him before. When it was time to sing she prayed: 'Lord Jesus sing through me this morning that the people might know you.' As she looked up she saw a bright garment fall on her shoulders and the power of God surged through her. Years later she understood from the Scriptures that what she prayed was for the anointing of the Holy Spirit. She believes that anointed and sanctified singers must learn to sing the Lord's song.

> His song demands the utmost commitment and faith. Born of the Word and inspired by the Spirit – the Song of the Lord issues forth from a heart unstained by pride and lust and constantly renouncing the spirit of the world.[76]

She mentions that the most important type of the song of the Lord is the song which God himself sings. It first belongs to God and proceeds from him and is therefore 'holy.' 'His song expresses his deepest love. His songs also minister deliverance in times of trouble. This primary expression is fundamental to any growth in ministering the songs of the Lord.'[77] Zephaniah 3: 14-17 describes the song of the Lord.

Sing O daughter of Zion! Shout O Israel! Be glad and
rejoice with all your heart O daughter of Jerusalem!
The Lord has taken away your judgments, He has
cast out your enemy. The King of Israel, the Lord is
in your midst: you shall see disaster no more. In that
day it shall be said to Jerusalem: 'Do not fear: Zion
let not your hands be weak. The Lord your God is in
your midst, the Mighty One will save: He will rejoice
over you with gladness, He will quiet you with His
love, He will rejoice over you with singing.

'In Hebrew the words in these verses for 'singing' and
'sing' paint a dynamic picture of the first characteristic of
God's song. They refer to a song that sounds like a loud
joyful cry of triumph. When God sings His song He is totally
uninhibited, extremely glad and bursting with absolute
triumph. And His song is filled with rejoicing. At the end
of verse 17 in the phrase 'rejoice over you with singing' –
the verb used is *'gil'* – a word that describes one of the most
radical expressions of joy in Scripture. It means 'to turn and
spin around in circles as if under the influence of strong
emotion.' God is extremely moved by the intense love He
has stirring in His heart for His people. In this passage
of Scripture we are commanded to sing all these radical
expressions of joy and triumph as this is a corporate song
of the Lord for His deliverance through Jesus!'[78] Tamara
believes the song of the Lord is born out of a right
relationship with God and originates from His song as it
is already real in the believer's heart: it is sung at the
appropriate time and is led and anointed by the Spirit: it is
often prophetic and prayer orientated:  it may be either pre-
written or spontaneous: it is Scriptural: and produces a deep
and lasting effect on the heart of the participant and
listener.[79]

Tamara shares a memorable experience of when she had to sing in front of around 1000 people. As she was quietly worshipping the anointing of God came upon her and she received two single words, but instinctively knew that a song of the Lord was about to be born. As she began to play on the piano words spontaneously poured forth and the room became saturated with the presence of God. The song lasted twenty minutes and 'suddenly as the Spirit of God began to move through the sanctuary, everyone unanimously without human prompting fell to their knees overwhelmed by the presence of Almighty God. Waves of God's glory swept back and forth throughout that place.'[80]

She believes one of the most interesting aspects of the song of the Lord His people sing to Him, is when there is a desire for renewal and the anointing of the Holy Spirit. When rivers of spiritual water have been blocked and need to be released again in a church or in individuals' lives, because of sin or where there is need for deliverance, the song of the Lord can release the blockage and set people free from their bondage. Churches or individuals can lose their spiritual vitality because of the 'foul play' of the enemy. Sadly, this can come from within the Christian community itself where there is jealousy or pride, or slander, and the Holy Spirit is grieved.[81]

The relevance of Tamara's testimony of the song of the Lord is that there is much more the Lord wants to do for His people in their corporate worship. As they acknowledge this and come with openness and humility before the Lord, He can take them into the ocean depths of worship that He desires to lead them into. Anointed praise and anointed worship, as well as anointed preaching are God's gifts to those who diligently seek Him with their whole heart, soul, mind and strength.

Examples of the song of the Lord in Scripture are Moses' song in Exodus 15: 1-18:

> I will sing unto the Lord for he has triumphed gloriously and the horse and his rider he has thrown into the sea. The Lord is my strength and my song and he has become my salvation: this is my God and I will praise Him, my father's God and I will exalt Him. (1-2)

> Who is like thee O Lord  among the nations?  Who is Like thee  majestic in  holiness, terrible in  glorious deeds doing wonders? (12)

Another example of the song of the Lord is Mary's song in Luke 1: 47-56 – The Magnificat:

> My soul magnifies the Lord and my spirit rejoices in God my Saviour, for he has regarded the low estate of his handmaiden. For behold from this day all generations will call me blessed: For He who is mighty has done great things for me and holy is His name. (47-48)

Yet another example of the song of the Lord is Handel's Messiah which hundreds of years after its miraculous birth can still be heard throughout the entire world. Handel was a man who had been granted the privilege of hearing one of the finest works of music ever to be sung for the glory of God. He was also a man who had learned to listen to the Lord's Song, as ministered to him by the Spirit and then communicated it to others – a small sample of heaven's song on earth.[82]

## CHAPTER SEVEN

## THE WISE SCRIBE

In Matthew's Gospel Jesus was teaching the crowds in parables about the kingdom of heaven when he said: 'Every scribe who has been trained for the kingdom of heaven is like a householder who brings out of his treasure what is new and old' – 13: 52. This is a helpful image especially for Anglicans because who we are has been shaped by our past. We do not think about contemporary and charismatic worship in a vacuum – because our roots have contributed to our formation and identity. (I am aware this chapter may be more relevant to Anglican worship).

Any minister seeking to enrich the worship of their church and help the congregation to learn more about contemporary or charismatic worship, can plan a preaching series and teach people about the dynamics, the flow, the philosophy, the theology and the vision for such worship. Having a resource library of books on this topic is also an invaluable tool for the church to learn from. To complement this home-groups can devote a term or two exploring the issue of worship.

### LITURGY
Those who are members of the Church of England will know that the dynamics and flow of their worship is likely to have an underlying liturgical shape to it. This will either be the Service of the Word or Holy Communion, even if these are only loosely adhered to. While those from a free-church background do not have a printed liturgical order for their worship, they still have an unwritten liturgical structure.

The term 'liturgy' may sound somewhat old-fashioned and be associated with traditional worship, but it is relevant to understand its proper meaning in worship. 'Liturgy comes from the Greek word *leitourgia* and is made up of words for work (*ergon*) and people (*laos*). In ancient Greece a liturgy was public work performed for the benefit of the city or state. Similarly, liturgy in worship is a work performed by the people for the benefit of others. It is the essence of the priesthood of all believers that the whole priestly community of Christians shares. To call a service 'liturgical' is to indicate that it was conceived so that all worshippers take an active part in offering their worship together. The word liturgy is used in the specific sense of the Eucharist, but Western Christians use *liturgical* to apply to all forms of public worship of a participatory nature. The concept of service then is fundamental to understanding worship.'[1]

Michael Perham has this to say about the use of liturgy in renewing our worship. 'Where a parish is coming alive the liturgy can be at the heart of it, can indeed be where renewal begins. Where people are finding their prayer life and their spirituality deepened, it can be because of the stimulus of liturgy where the Spirit can move among the worshippers. Where the church has the opportunity to reach out into the community in a special service to mark a great occasion or a national disaster, it is better equipped to do so because every community and every worship leader, has had the experience of being liturgically creative.'[2]

Maggi Dawn, a former professional musician, singer and now Chaplain at Robinson College in Cambridge, continues to write on the theology and practice of contemporary liturgy. She comments on the use of rite and liturgy in worship where 'rite' refers to recognised and constantly repeated forms of Christian worship, within both liturgical and non-liturgical traditions. 'I am fairly certain that much of what is going on in the experimental edge of worship will, sooner or later, serve to reshape the rite of the church. But while I welcome innovation I do not believe that it should replace the best of traditional worship, but that the two should inform each other. I would suggest that the way forward is neither to replace tradition with innovation, nor to adapt traditional services by inserting extra bits in the hope of making them relevant, but to allow different forms of rite to exist side by side. In other words let's abandon the 'variety show' approach to worship and dare to extend our repertoire of rite, performing each within chosen limits in order to maintain an integrity of form. Our rites will stand a better chance of fulfilling their purpose – not merely to perpetuate a tradition, but to create a context where people can engage with God.'[3]

## COMMUNION

The Rev. Dr. C. Cocksworth, the Principal of Ridley Hall in Cambridge, is happy to be quoted as saying – 'he considers the Communion Service is the best setting for charismatic worship.' As an Anglican Minister I believe Evangelical charismatics should celebrate Communion more often, as they only tend to do this once a month at their main Sunday Service. The advantage of Communion is that it has a well-balanced structure of word and sacrament and contains substantial biblical content. It can include clusters of sung worship and room for spontaneity. It can have space to wait for the Holy Spirit to move and also for God's people to use their gifts. On occasions this can involve sharing testimonies of what the Lord has done for them.

C. Cocksworth draws our attention to the fact that at 'The Reformation, Archbishop Cranmer like other great reformers such as Martin Luther, Martin Bucer and John Calvin desired a weekly Communion Service. Cranmer's pattern gave full expression to the need to be fed by Scripture and Sacrament. Holy Communion has always centered on the presence of Jesus with his people and continually keeps before the Church the central acts of our redemption – the dying and rising of Jesus. With this comes an appreciation of the cost of our redemption as well as the benefits that we have received, so that the natural response is one of gratitude – the loving thankfulness of those who know themselves to be bought with a price by an act of God's sheer generosity and love'[4]

We should not forget that Jesus himself commanded us at the Last Supper to – 'do this in remembrance of me' – Matt. 26: 26-28. The Communion Service is the place where the presence of Christ is experienced in an intimate way. This should strongly appeal to those who are especially keen on intimacy in contemporary worship. Michael Ramsey former Archbishop of Canterbury says:

> Mystery means that Christ by his body and his blood feeds his people with himself...[6]

Peter Atkins in 'Memory And Liturgy' draws our attention to Christ's words in the Eucharist. He points out the best way to understand words in another language is to see the context in which they are used on various occasions, and also the associated ideas that are linked to those words. 'To remember is to link past, present and future in a single fold. The brain has this fantastic capacity to work in a multi-time zone without losing touch (if it is functioning normally) with the reality of time. I can make the past present, and I can imagine the future now, while at the same time remaining aware of the 'history' of the past and the 'image' of the future.' In effect we can recall the presence of Christ at this moment while also recognising Jesus is part of history – and that his presence foreshadows his coming again in the future.[6] 'To re-member is to re-embody, to bring together, to bring alive, that which is past, and to make it effective in the present and for the future...Through the faculty of memory the person remembered can 'come alive again.'[7]

Bishop A. T. John Robinson writing in 'Liturgy Coming to Life' almost fifty years ago, was innovative in his vision of the relevance of liturgy to life. Speaking about the relevance

of the Parish Communion within the life of the church and in
the world he concluded:

> It was then for the first time that I saw the essential
> connection between liturgy and evangelism...It was
> not liturgical reform for its own sake or in isolation
> from the rest of the life of the worshipping,
> witnessing and healing Community...The sharing
> of Bread must be continued socially – and thence
> economically and politically...Holy Communion is
> the great workshop of the new world...Liturgy is at
> its heart social action, the point where this world is
> taken and consecrated, broken and restored for God
> and his Kingdom, and where the Church itself is
> renewed as the agent of Christian revolution.[8]

These words still have a prophetic and revolutionary note at
the beginning of the 21st century – because they challenge us
to interpret our worship in the context of all of life – and to
embrace the whole of life within it too.

D. Gregory Dix reminds us of the four actions of the
Communion Service. 'The offertory, bread and wine are
'taken' and placed on the table together. The prayer, the
president gives thanks to God over the bread and wine
together. The fraction, the bread is broken. The Communion,
the bread and wine are distributed together.'[9] 'The Eucharist
is an action – 'do this' – with a particular meaning given to it
by our Lord himself.'[10]And that meaning refers to his body
and blood given for us on the cross. But, it also embraces a
simple yet profound symbolism. In the gospel accounts:
'Jesus took: he blessed: he broke: he gave.' This is the
symbolic action of the Eucharist when Jesus gave thanks for
the bread and the wine – and when we give thanks for his
broken body and shed blood. God still seeks servants to
follow Christ and worship Him – God then 'shapes them
eucharistically' – as he takes them and blesses them and

metaphorically breaks them, and through them nourishes others with Christ.

We not only focus on the presence of Christ in Holy Communion but also on the presence of God amongst his people. C. Cocksworth reminds us that the priority of David Watson was the recovery of the power of the presence of God, shown by the signs of the presence of his power (sacraments), leading to the praise of his people (eucharist) in their life together (fellowship). He also brings to our attention that: 'Evangelical Charismatics discovered that the activity of the Spirit in the present moment often occurred in a eucharistic setting. David Watson detailed conversions, re-dedications, convictions of sin, healing and filling of the Spirit in the context of the Sacrament (Communion). Michael Green considered the Communion Service to be the appropriate place for the exercise of spiritual gifts. Similarly David Pytches advised those who permitted the use of spiritual gifts to expect to see them manifested within the Eucharist.'[11]

## INFORMALITY

One of the characteristic features of contemporary and charismatic worship is the informal atmosphere and the casual dress of those leading. Perhaps those who embrace this style do so because it is 'cool' and appeals to young people and young adults who identify with it. As a minister who was formerly in fashion I am inclined to think that those who lead public worship should dress up rather than down. What is the casual and informal style of leading saying about God, our faith and our approach in worship? What is the philosophy and theology behind this model that gives it its contemporary appeal? Mark Ashton, the Vicar of the Round Church in Cambridge, highlights the impression of superficiality that may well inadvertently be communicated when leading services in an informal manner. 'The person leading the service must seek to achieve a balance between gripping the interest and attention of the congregation, and communicating the seriousness of what is happening. Some service leading is good at holding attention but communicates a sense of superficiality.' [12]

In this informal context the person leading worship can in some instances be likened to a compere fronting a show. This can border on entertaining the congregation although there is nothing novel in this approach. Twenty-five years ago an Anglican minister I knew well, discarded his clerical robes and collar and led services in a suit in an informal manner. At the time this was a rather radical approach. But the atmosphere felt more like entertainment than worship. David Stancliffe the Bishop of Salisbury says:

> I mind a lot about worship and wonder at the quality of what is offered in some places in this most important area of the Church's life. In an age when the standards of public performance are so high, how do worshippers manage to keep on going to church faithfully when the way the worship is prepared and offered is often so dire: when it is frequently confused with entertainment and when it is led by those who apparently have no idea about what they are doing, or professional competence in doing it? [13]

Those accustomed to an informal style of worship may feel this is somewhat of a caricature and overlooks the fact it may be considered to be culturally relevant. But, there can be a downside to this as at times it can feel as if our worship is being dumbed down. If the theology behind the informal approach is an attempt to embrace the immanence of God, we have to ask ourselves to what extent it cloaks his transcendence?' We may be 'chummy' with God in our colloquial chats with him, but leading worship in this way can lead to complacency and a lack of reverence. Bearing in mind the attention to detail God required of worship in the Old Testament, (see Ch. 1), is it time to reflect on the ethos our informal style of worship embraces? It may be also be a timely reminder that a more formal manner of leading services, albeit in an informal setting, may reflect a more respectful approach in our worship. While this may sound too traditional it may help to express a more noticeably overt sense of reverence.

## THE SANCTUARY – STAGE

In contemporary worship the sanctuary-stage is likely to be inundated with musicians, their instruments, microphones and overhead projectors. There may be no furniture such as a lectern, or pulpit, or a communion table of any artistic merit or substance that catches our attention. To what extent does this help us to focus on the Lord as the object of our worship? Gone is the Old Testament model of the sanctuary reminding us of the presence of God and being a symbol of a 'sacred space.' This would now be difficult as we have crowded out the Lord in the sanctuary-stage. One alternative to cluttering this with musicians, their instruments and other technology, is to move them to one side even if this means making room for them. We can experiment and dispense with overhead projectors and have a modern hymnbook, along with a contemporary songbook we have put together that can easily be updated.

Michael Perham speaks about the importance of the sanctuary and its furniture, when he reminds us that in our busy cluttered lives physical space in the sanctuary can be a 'holy space.' He also says:

> Because it is the place where we focus the presence of Christ in the liturgy, the altar has itself become for many a sacrament of Christ and his presence in the Church...Because of all the experiences of the presence of Christ among his people in worship, his presence in the bread and wine which they consecrate

and share is the most telling. The altar table becomes
for many the ultimate sign of Christ's presence in
every act of liturgical worship and in the church
building itself.[14]

As we celebrate Christ's presence in a traditional Eucharist it
is usual for God's people to come and kneel at the altar rail
to receive Communion. In contemporary worship people can
be invited to come and kneel at the altar rail to receive
Communion. This can be a moving symbol of humility and
reverence that brings a balance in our informal approach.

## SILENCE

M. Perham mentions the clutter and busyness of our lives
and in worship we may also find we are bombarded with
stressful levels of loud music. This reminds us that silence is
an essential and integral aspect of worship. Silence can help
us gather our thoughts at the beginning of a service to be
aware of God's presence. Silence before the confession and
after the absolution can help us to take in God's forgiveness.
Silence after the Scripture readings and the sermon is also
helpful as we respond to hearing God speak to us through
His Word. Silence is also appropriate when we have sung
our worship songs and have sensed the stillness of God's
presence amongst us.

Tim Hughes shares a memorable experience of silence in
worship in the township of Inanda, Durban in South Africa.
'It was a hot and humid Sunday. Sweat was pouring down
my face and the service hadn't even begun.The congregation
was gathering but as I looked to the front of the church I
was perplexed to see no drums, no amps, no keyboards. I
wondered how on earth we were going to worship. And then
it began. A loud voice pierced the silence and instantly
all the people were on their feet singing their hearts out. The
harmonies and melodies that filled the air created the most
beautiful sound. The joy and heartfelt adoration on the faces
of the congregation was infectious. I wanted what they had.

Here were people wholeheartedly consumed with their Saviour. They had a joy and contentment that made me envious. Yet when I looked at their surroundings I was confused. The people of this township live in extreme poverty. AIDS is rife and pain and suffering are part of everyday life. Surely their songs should be those of lament and pain not joy and celebration? It took a while to sink in but as the service progressed the reason for their joy struck me. They had encountered the Lord Jesus. They knew where they had come from: they were well aware of their present, but ultimately they understood where they were going. Whatever life threw at them it couldn't rob them of the glorious riches of knowing God and being known by Him. They would always have reason to praise. That Sunday morning I learnt an invaluable lesson about worship. Worship is not about songs or music. Worship is all about Jesus.[15]

From this memorable encounter we can see there is room for sung worship without a band always playing loud music. What also stands out is that the deeper God's people are led to encounter Him and the Lord Jesus in their lives – the more their worship will reflect the depth and the reality of the worship of this impoverished township.

## PROCLAMATION & PRAYER

In contemporary worship the lectern may be nothing more than a music stand that may also be used as a pulpit. Yet liturgically there is a symbolic significance attached to it. A proper lectern is more than just a place to put our notes on especially if it also doubles as a pulpit. It speaks about the importance of Scripture along with the central place of preaching the Word of God. For instance, to have a solid oak or ash lectern/pulpit signifies the authority of God's Word as it is read and expounded.

One of the most surprising things about Evangelical worship, in both traditional and contemporary services, is the custom to have only one reading of Scripture. The impact of God's Word is not solely confined to preaching but can be just as powerful when read out aloud – as this allows the Lord to speak directly through His Word to His people. Is it time to elevate the reading of God's Word and to have three Scripture readings: one from the Old Testament, one from the New Testament and a Psalm? Or one from the Old Testament, one from the New Testament and a Gospel reading? A eucharistic church would invariably include three readings. God's Word has an intrinsic authority as it is read out aloud and it enhances our worship when we include more scripture readings. To do this would also increase the biblical content of our worship.

In contemporary worship the prayers can often fall into the pattern of an informal style that is much more suitable in personal prayer. One long informal prayer often embraces all the topics without any response for the congregation to participate in. The traditional manner of leading public prayer as is found in Anglican Common Worship is a much more suitable model. This style allows different topics for prayer to be introduced and invites the congregation's participation with the words: 'Lord in your mercy – Hear our prayer.' This model also allows silence to be included in-between topics.

## THE GATHERING
In the Communion Service in Anglican worship the beginning is called 'the gathering' but in contemporary worship people may not be aware of the importance of this concept, which is a time for preparing our hearts to worship the Lord. A Service of the Word also has a time of preparation at the start similar to the concept of 'the gathering.' People of all ages come to church and bring the impact of their week with them. Some will come with joyful,

thankful hearts. Others will come burdened and yet others may have been hassled getting their children ready. Michael Perham points out that people arrive at church as individuals with their own needs, and are expected to be part of a congregation with people they may not know, and perhaps with people they may have not seen since last Sunday.

> The gathering is a recognition that we need binding together with our neigbours if we are genuinely to be a congregation and the body of Christ. We need gathering time to prepare. We need to get ready for communication with God. We need to begin to understand what it is that we are specifically gathering to celebrate. In some churches today people prepare for worship by the singing of songs and choruses for a time before the 'service proper begins.' It is a recognition of the same thing that liturgy has always nearly seen – that we need time to warm up – to God, to each other and to what we are to celebrate.[16]

While the concept of gathering the congregation is clear – in practice this may not necessarily be how the worship begins. The welcome and notices can often take quite a few minutes before the service starts. However, where there is a worship group the members can start singing about 10 minutes before the service begins. This reinforces the idea of getting ready to worship the Lord and songs can be chosen that help people to prepare their hearts.

I have observed in churches with eucharistic worship, the minister is unlikely to go through all the notices that are already printed on a sheet. Yet some churches can take a few minutes announcing events listed in the notice sheet. A warm effusive welcome to everyone including visitors, with a brief announcement of the theme of the worship is all that is required at the start of the service. Whatever we do at the beginning should be with the aim of helping people to prepare their hearts to worship the Lord. If we want to mention any notices this can be done by briefly drawing attention to them either at the beginning, or even the end of the service when people are more likely to remember them.

How we begin our worship should primarily be geared to focusing peoples' attention onto the Lord. So it is important to teach that the beginning of the service is really where the worship does begin and not when we start having 'a time of sung worship.' After the minister has welcomed everyone he can invite the congregation to stand in God's presence and read some verses of Scripture accompanied by prayer that invokes God's blessing on the worship. Creative ways of leading the first part of the Service can then be implemented each week.

## CORPORATE CONFESSION

In contemporary worship the confession and absolution tend to be over very quickly and do not have much biblical content. Equally, when a confession is used that someone has composed this also usually lacks substance. It is of interest to note what two well known liturgists have to say about the confession. 'Penitence ought nearly always to be part of our approach to Communion but on occasions it should be brief and to the point – while on other occasions we should be prepared to give more time and space to this element in our worship' – Michael Perham, the Bishop of Gloucester.[17] 'The confession of sin is regarded by many as the center of penitence but the gospel is about forgiveness which means that the absolution, the declaration of forgiveness puts the seal on this important preliminary. It is not about grovelling. It is about a sober view of ourselves...It is in this spirit that we come to confess' – Kenneth Stevenson, the Bishop of Portsmouth.[18]

The confession has three component parts and it is helpful to bear these in mind when leading others in this act of worship: 1/ 'The biblical injunction to confess: 2/ the right attitude of confession, humble, penitent, obedient, honest: 3/ the character of God – He is Almighty seated on a royal throne: but is also a heavenly Father, of infinite goodness and mercy, gracious and ready to forgive.'[19] It may well be helpful to those leading worship to use these principles as a guideline for choosing or writing a corporate confession – and also to ensure that the content is biblically substantial.

If the confession and absolution come at the beginning of the Service, sufficient time has to be given to prepare peoples' hearts so they can meaningfully participate. For Anglicans the confession from the Communion Service can be used. I myself love the 'Collect for Purity' that can also be lifted out and used independently. For instance, this can be sung 2-3 times before the confession and can be followed by verses of Scripture that remind us of God's forgiveness. Alternatively, 'Your Blood Speaks' by Matt Redman (No: 150 S. S. 2006), or 'By Your Blood' (Hosanna Music 1991) can be sung. After this silence allows the Holy Spirit to search peoples' hearts so they can participate meaningfully in the corporate confession. Equally, verses of Scripture can be read as part of the preparation before the confession. The opportunity can be taken to vary where the confession comes. Sometimes it may be appropriate to have this as part of the intercessions or after the sermon. On occasions, after the absolution, a song can express the gratitude in peoples' hearts for God's forgiveness. Ensuring the confession and absolution is a substantial act of worship, allows the Lord to minister to those whose hearts are burdened by the guilt of their sin and remind us of the holy God we come to worship.

Just as on occasions when there is a healing service people can come forward and kneel to receive prayer – I am inclined to think that there should also be the opportunity for people to come forward and kneel as an act of penitence. This may be valued when they are burdened by guilt or have been through a phase when they have struggled with temptation and sin in their lives. There may also be those who would value this because their failure in the past still troubles them. In the silence of their hearts as they kneel they can confess their failure or sin to the Lord, after which the minister can pronounce God's forgiveness. Alternatively, they may wish to read out a prayer of confession and then receive God's forgiveness. This can be very meaningful if the corporate confession and absolution is not dealing with their feelings of condemnation, failure or guilt. To include this act of public penitence allows a corporate identity and solidarity with those individuals who go forward. It is also a sign the Christian community has acknowledged Christ's forgiveness to them. This has the potential to be a very meaningful and powerful part of our worship. I myself as a minister would value the opportunity to go forward in an act of public penitence.

## SUNG WORSHIP

At the charismatic Assemblies Of God in Nottingham in the mid 80s, when I occasionally worshipped there with my wife, the same person led the sung worship that lasted 45 minutes. Often songs were repeated a number of times, but the leader was sensitive and skilled in leading us into God's presence and allowing us to remain there. He also avoided any emotional hype or manipulation. In contemporary sung worship the gift of leading people into God's presence, and discerning when we have entered His presence, and allowing God's people to remain there – is a gift to be coveted and developed.

In a large congregation there may be a number of bands that lead sung worship in rotation. Although this involves more musicians it can make it difficult for the congregation to establish a rapport with them as there is a different band each week. If there was only one band with the most gifted and anointed musicians, how much more would this enhance the worship? This can also introduce a greater emphasis on the quality of the musicians and how well they complement each other. Having only one worship band may also help them to establish a rapport with the congregation and acquire a sensitivity to what God is doing amongst them. Would this enable the band to grow together and mature in leading God's people in worship? This need not sideline other musicians as in a large church there would be other opportunities for them. Singers or a choir whose gifting and anointing is to lead the congregation in sung worship, can also work in harmony with the band.

## LEADING SERVICES

In large churches alongside the clergy there may also be a number of lay people leading the Sunday Services. The challenge is to be open and sensitive to what the Lord may be doing amongst His people as they lead the congregation in worship. One advantage for ministers is that they have more experience in this area. Also one aspect of their call is to devote time to plan and prepare and pray about the worship and how it develops. As the benchmark for leading worship C. Cocksworth has some insightful comments.

> Good presiders 'feel the freedom' of their role. They know their way around the liturgy. They feel the pulse of the people. They listen for the breath of God. They can move with the dynamics of worship giving space for spontaneity, room for silence and are trusted by their people to lead them towards moments of encounter with Christ, the head of the body.[20]

Tim Hughes gives an example of such leadership by Mike Pilavachi that memorably affected the outcome of their worship. 'I remember a time a few years ago when I was leading worship at an event in the north east of England. There were about a thousand young people packed into the tent. As I came to what I thought was the end of the worship I turned to Mike who was leading the service and waited for him to end in prayer and speak. Instead he suggested we wait as he felt there was something more to happen. We waited for a while and then started singing the simple refrain: 'Praise the Lord O my soul praise the Lord.' After a while the band stopped but the young people continued to sing. The band left the stage and Mike and I sat at the side and joined in with everyone. What happened next was amazing. There was a hushed silence and then someone started another song. This was followed by a time of singing in the Spirit. Then people started cheering and shouting out praise to God. Again there was a holy silence and after a while new melodies and songs started to fill the air. We had an incredible time responding to God and the floodgates of heaven opened. God poured out his Spirit in a very powerful way. We worshipped like this for at least 45 minutes and the wonderful thing was that no one was on stage leading it. The Holy Spirit was leading it. There was no one telling us what to do next. The Holy Spirit was leading us and a thousand young people joined together in response. It was a night I will never forget and it reminded me of the need to lead God's way. Sometimes that means getting out of the way and making space for God to work.'[21]

## THE HOLY SPIRIT

This highlights that when we are open and sensitive to the Holy Spirit in our worship the Lord will move among His people possibly in unexpected ways. So it is prudent to allow space in our worship for the Lord to move in this way. We see an example of this in the life of the church at Antioch in Acts ch. 13. Here Luke presents us with the briefest cameo of this church at worship. David Williams says: 'The word translated worshipping is that usually employed in the LXX for the service of priests and Levites in the temple (Greek *Leitourgein*-our 'liturgy').[22] We can assume all the members of the church attended this formal act of worship when one of the main aspects on that day was fasting. The significance of this is seen as they waited expectantly on the Lord to hear what He had to say. Prayer was undoubtedly included in their worship as they fasted – a sign of the church's trust in the Lord to guide and direct them.

On that particular day the Lord spoke through the Holy Spirit and gave them what was to prove to be a historically important message: 'Set apart for me Barnabas and Saul for the work to which I have called them.' As evangelists they were soon to embark on their first missionary journey. This word from the Lord through the Spirit, is reported in a matter of fact way, and indicates the church was used to the Lord speaking to them in this way. We would describe this as a charismatic church that used spiritual gifts as an integral part of their worship. What is striking is that churches who identify themselves as charismatic often do not make space in worship for the Lord to spontaneously speak to them through the Holy Spirit.

The church at Antioch teaches to us to make time in our worship to listen to the Lord and expect him to speak to us through the Holy Spirit. Clearly this church was used to spending time in prayer and fasting before the Lord: had faith He would speak: were secure in allowing the Holy Spirit freedom in worship – and submitted themselves as a church to the authority and Lordship of Christ. Subsequently, He spoke to them through the Holy Spirit and this was significant in spreading the gospel. In the context of their charismatic worship we can reasonably assume, that one of the prophets had a word of knowledge from the Lord laid on their heart or mind by the Holy Spirit. Acts ch. 13: 3 indicates that further fasting and prayer took place probably over a period of time, after which the church confirmed the call of Barnabas and Saul.

A SOCIOLOGICAL PERSPECTIVE

Martin Stringer a lecturer in Sociology and Anthropology and Head of Theology and Religious Studies at Birmingham University, in his recent book – 'A Sociological History Of Christian Worship' – develops the idea of a discourse as a way of understanding Christian worship within its many and diverse social contexts. He does so by exploring worship around the world from the early church up until the year 2000. His conclusions are striking.

As he reflects on his research, he submits that if 'the meal' –the Eucharist and the Holy Spirit could ever be successfully reunited, then Christian worship could be launched again in a new round of renewal. He also suggests that such renewal has to embrace charity, giving and supporting the poor and the oppressed. He observes that the language of sacrifice has almost gone from many contemporary discourses almost with good reason – but that the voluntary laying down of our lives, metaphorically or in reality, for God and for our friends is an important part of the Christian discourse. He is convinced the comfortableness and the illusion of intimacy is the gravest danger faced by contemporary Western liturgy:

> I have noticed in both England and the United States an increasing sense of comfortableness and intimacy in contemporary worship that stretches across the traditions: carpets on the floor, a crèche for the children, power-point technology providing reassuring images, language that does not offend and music aimed to speak to our emotions and calm us down. This clearly reflects contemporary global society and the discourses of consumerism and individual well-being that dominate it – but is this truly Christian?[23]

# FOOTNOTES

## INTRODUCTION

1.   J. Gledhill  Leading A Local Church – In The Age Of The Spirit  SPCK  2003  38
2.   G. Kendrick  Worship  Kingsway  1984  23
3.   D. Peterson  Engaging With God – A Biblical Theology Of Worship  Apollos  1992  17
4.   Ibid  19
5.   Ibid  46
6.   M. Dawn  Reaching Out Without Dumbing Down quoting W. Temple  Eerdmans  1995  80
7.   C. Cocksworth  Holy, Holy, Holy – Worshipping The Trinitarian God  DLT  2004  32-33
8.   J. F. White  Christian Worship  Abingdon  1986 17
9.   Ibid  17
10.  C. Cocksworth  ibid  145, 163
11.  Ibid  189-190
12.  Ibid  191
13.  T. A. Dearborn & S. Coil  Worship At The Next Level  Baker  2004  11
14   Ibid  12
15.  D. F. Ford & D. W. Hardy  Living In Praise  DLT  2005  8
16.  Ibid  8-9
17.  Ibid  64
18.  Ibid  64-65
19.  Ibid  65-66

## CHAPTER ONE

1.   D. Peterson  ibid  23
2.   A. Hill  Enter His Courts With Praise  Kingsway  1998  32
3.   Ibid  32
4.   Ibid  32-33

5.      C. Westermann  Genesis Ch. 12-36  Fortress Press
        1995  356
6.      W. Brueggemann  Genesis  J. Knox Press  1982  185
7.      Ibid  187
8.      V. P. Hamilton  Genesis Ch. 18-50  Eerdmans  1995
        99
9.      Ibid  99-102
10.     Ibid  103-104, 107
11.     M. Redman  Facedown  Kingsway  2005  29
12.     M. J. Selman  Sacrifice In The Bible  Editors R. T.
        Beckwith & M. J. Selman  Baker  1995  158
13.     D. Peterson  ibid  24
14.     T. E. Fretheim  Exodus  J. Knox Press  1991
        264-265
15.     A. Motyer  Exodus  IVP  2005  250
16.     M. Redman  ibid  29
17.     A. Motyer  ibid  267
18.     T. E. Fretheim  Ibid  216-219
19.     Ibid  315
20.     A. Hill  ibid  3-4, 13
21.     D. Zscech  Extravagant Worship  Bethany House
        2002  80
22.     A. Hill  ibid  121-122
23.     Ibid  122-125
24.     B. Childs  Exodus  SCM  1987  564
25.     T. E Fretheim  ibid  281-282
26.     B. Childs  ibid  566
27.     Ibid  542-543
28.     T. E. Fretheim  ibid  280-281
29.     G. Wenham  Leviticus  Eerdmans  1979  129
30.     Ibid  26
31.     Ibid  27
32.     W. H. Bellinger Jr.  Leviticus  Paternoster  2001  99
33      Ibid  100
34.     Ibid  100
35.     ibid  101
36.     P. Jensen  Sacrifice In The Bible  ibid  37

## CHAPTER TWO

1. W. Brueggemann Jeremiah Eerdmans 1998 36
2. Brueggemann quoting A Welch ibid 36
3. Ibid 39
4. Ibid 78
5. Ibid 79-80
6. D. J. Simundson Amos Abingdon 2005 164
7. Ibid 188-189
8. J. L. Mays Amos SCM 1969 106-107
9. J. A. Motyer Amos BST 1974 131

## CHAPTER THREE

1. M. Ashton in Worship By The Book Editor D. A. Carson Zondervann 2002 82
2. C. G. Broyles Psalms Paternoster 2002 2-3, 7-9, 11
3. P. Westermeyer Te Deum – The Church & Music Fortress Press 1998 34-35
4. J. L. Mays Psalms J Knox Press 1994 1
5. Ibid 1
6. Ibid 1
7. P. Westermeyer ibid 24
8. Ibid 7
9. W. Brueggemann The Message Of The Psalms Augsburg 1984 15
10. W. Brueggemann The Psalms – The Life Of Faith Fortress Press 1995 101-102
11. Ibid 102-103
12. P. Ward Selling Worship Abingdon 2005 204
13. Ibid 107
14. P. Westermeyer ibid 26
15. C. Croeker Music In Christian Worship Liturgical Press 2005 77-78
16. R. Redman The Great Worship Awakening Jossey-Bass 2002 26
17. P. Westermeyer ibid 30

18.    W. Brueggemann  Israel's Praise  Fortress Press
       1988  4
19.    Ibid  11
20.    A. Weiser  Psalms  J. Knox Press 1962  219
21.    C. Westermann  Praise & Lament In The Psalms
       J. Knox  Press  1981  52
22.    A. Weiser  ibid  224-225
23.    J. L. Mays  ibid  105-106
24.    Ibid  113-115

**CHAPTER FOUR**

1.     P. O'Brien  Philippians  Eerdmans  1991  388-389
2.     Hawthorn: Martin: Reid Dictionary of Paul & His
       Letters  IVP  1993  562
3.     M. Hooker  Paul A Short Introduction  Oneworld
       Oxford  2004  50-51
4.     J. D. G. Dunn  The Theology Of Paul The Apostle
       Eerdmans  1998  251-254
5.     P. O'Brien  ibid  232-234
6.     G. Fee  ibid  222-223
7.     Ibid  224
8.     P. O'Brien  ibid  238, 241
9.     D. Peterson  Ibid  253
10.    F. F. Bruce  Hebrews  Eerdmans  1990  57-58
11.    Ibid  31
12.    Ibid  30-31
13.    R. Brown  Hebrews  IVP  1982  93-94
14.    Ibid  quoting  A. T. H. Robinson  96
15.    P. Ellingworth  Hebrews  Eerdmans  1993  268
16.    C. R. Koester  Hebrews  Anchor  2001  283, 293
17.    R. Brown  ibid  100
18.    F.F. Bruce  ibid  131
19.    C. R. Koester  ibid  299
20.    F. F. Bruce  ibid  185-186
21.    R. Brown  ibid  152

22.  W. Nee The Normal Christian Life  Kingsway  1989 13-14
23.  R.C. Moberly Ministerial Priesthood  J. Murray  1899 245
24.  Ibid  246
25.  I. Bradley  The Power Of Sacrifice  DLT  1995  284
26.  Ibid  quoting Charles Wesley  261
27.  F. F. Bruce  ibid  339
28.  C. Gray  The Fire & The Clay  Guiver et al  SPCK 1999  48
29.  Ibid  49
30.  C. Cocksworth & R. Brown  Being A Priest Today Canterbury Press  2002  6-7
31.  M. Ramsey  The Christian Priest Today  SPCK  1987 106-107
32.  P. H. Davids  1 Peter  Eerdmans  1990  87
33.  T. R. Schreiner  1& 2 Peter  Broadman & Holman 2003  105
34.  Ibid  106

**CHAPTER FIVE**

1.  M. Redman  Facedown  Kingsway  2004  18-20
2.  J. N. Oswalt  Isaiah Ch. 1-39  Eerdmans  1986  180
3.  B. S. Childs  Isaiah  J. Knox Press  2002  55
4.  J. N. Oswalt  ibid  176
5.  Ibid  177
6.  W. Brueggemann  Isaiah Ch. 1-39  J. Knox Press 1998  58-59
7.  J. N. Oswalt  ibid  180
8.  W. Brueggemann  ibid  59-60
9.  J. N. Oswalt  ibid  185
10.  B. Childs  ibid  56
11.  W. Eichrodt  Ezekiel  Westminster Press 1970  2, 4
12.  D. L. Block  Ezekiel Ch. 1-24  Eerdmans  1997  87
13.  J. Blenkinsopp  Ezekiel  J. Knox Press  1990  16
14.  C. J. H. Wright  Ezekiel  IVP  2001  22-23

15.    W. Eichrodt ibid 53-54
16.    C. J. H. Wright ibid 24-26
17.    Ibid 51
18.    Ibid 51-52
19.    D. L. Block ibid 96
20.    Ibid 97
21.    Ibid 105
22.    Ibid 109
23.    G. E. Ladd Revelation Eerdman 1972 7-9
24.    M. E. Boring Revelation J. Knox Press 1989 5-7
25.    D. A. Carson ibid 23
26.    I. Boxhall Revelation Continuum 2006 83-84
27.    Ibid 85
28.    Ibid 86
29.    G. E. Ladd ibid 77
30.    I. Boxall ibid 89
31.    Ibid 99
32.    Ibid 101-102
33.    N. Due Created For Worship Mentor 2005 222
34.    M. E. Boring ibid 193

## CHAPTER SIX

1.    Q. J. Schultze High-Tech Worship Baker 2000 20
2.    Ibid 23, 26-27
3.    T. & J. Wright Contemporary Worship Abingdon
      1997 23-24
4.    Ibid 21
5.    C. Plantinga Jr. & S. A. Rozeboom Discerning The
      Spirits Eerdmans 2003 3
6.    P. Ward ibid 2005 70-72
7.    J. Steven Worship In The Restoration Movement
      Grove 1989 3-4, 9-11
8.    R. Redman ibid 34-35
9.    Ibid 36
10.   A. Park To Know You More Kingsway 2002
      319-320

11. Ibid 320-321
12 Ibid 317
13. Ibid 312-313
14. Ibid 321-322
15. J. Leach Liturgy & Liberty Marc 1992 152-153
16. P. Oakley Soul Survivor Songbook 2001 Article in Index
17. P. Hocken Streams Of Renewal –The Origins & Early Development Of The Charismatic Movement Paternoster 1997 148-149
18. Ibid 149-150
19. Ibid 149-151
20. Ibid 159-165
21. Ibid 64
22. P. Ward ibid 152
23. Ibid 16
24. Ibid 17
25. M. Pilavachi For The Audience Of One Hodder 1999 134-135
26. D. Lucarni Why I Left The Contemporary Christian Music Movement Evangelical Press 2002 52
27. Ibid 68
28 Ibid 53-55
29. Ibid 58-59
30. R. Redman Ibid 47-48
31. Ibid 54-55
32. Ibid 57
33. Ibid 61,67,71
34. M.Redman The Unquenchable Worshipper Kingsway 2001 29
35. N. Page And Now For A Time Of Nonsense Continuum 2004 2
36. M. Redman Article in Index Soul Survivor Songbook 2001
37. N. Page ibid 37-38
38. P. Moger Music & Worship: Principles To Practice Grove 1994 14, 18-19

39.    D. A. Carson  John  IVP  1991  225
40.    C. K. Barrett  John  Westminster Press  237, 239
41.    L. Morris  John  Eerdmans  1995  240
42.    R. E. Brown  John Ch. 1-12  Anchor  1966  180
43.    J. M. Boice John Vol 1 Ch. 1-4  Baker  2000  298
44.    Ibid  296
45.    J. R. Watson  Hymns  OUP  2003  6
46.    P. Westermeyer  ibid  202
47.    J. R. Watson  ibid  164
48.    Ibid  12,15
49.    P. Westermeyer  ibid  202
50.    J. R. Watson  ibid  205-208
51.    Ibid  207
52.    C. Cocksworth  Evangelical Eucharistic Thought In
       The 20th Century  CUP  2002  63-66
53.    D. Stancliffe  God's Pattern – Shaping Our Worship,
       Ministry & Life  SPCK  2003  40
54.    N. Page  ibid  42-43
55.    P. Oakley  Article in Index  Soul Survivor Songbook
       2001
56.    D. Zscech  ibid  26
57.    T. Hughes  Passion For Your Name  Kingsway
       2003  84
58.    P. Ward  ibid  209-210
59.    C. Cocksworth Holding Together Catholic
       Evangelical Worship In The Spirit – Lecture in Anvil
       2005 7,13
60.    R. Parry  Worshipping Trinity  Continuum  2005  1-2
61.    Ibid  110-111
62.    Ibid  109
63.    J. H. S. Steven  Worship In The Spirit – Charismatic
       Worship In The Church Of England  Paternoster
       2002  132-133
64.    Ibid  133
65.    Ibid  188-189
66.    Ibid  192
67.    Ibid  193-194

68.   Ibid  194-196
69.   Ibid  197
70.   Ibid  199
71.   T. Smail, Walker, Wright  Charismatic Renewal
      SPCK  1993  112
72.   Ibid  111
73.   Ibid  110
74.   M. Redman  ibid  22
75.   Ibid  45
76.   T. Winslow  The Song Of The Lord  Kingsway  1996
      9-11
77.   Ibid  15
78    Ibid  22-23
79.   Ibid  17
80.   Ibid  19-20
81.   Ibid  60-61
82.   Ibid  85-86

## CHAPTER SEVEN

1.    T. A. Dearborn & S. Coil  ibid  25
2.    M. Perham  New Handbook Of Pastoral Liturgy
      SPCK  2000  12
3.    P. Ward Editor The Rite Stuff  Article by M. Dawn
      BRF  2004  25, 36
4.    D. Kennedy  Understanding Anglican Worship
      Grove  1997  6-7
5.    K. Stevenson  Do this – The Shape, Meaning & Style
      Of The Eucharist  Canterbury Press  202 quoting
      M. Ramsey  63
6.    P. Atkins  Memory & Liturgy  Ashgate  2004  X-X1
7.    J. A. T Robinson quoted by E. James – A Life Of
      Bishop John A T. Robinson  Collins  1987  55
8.    P. Atkins  ibid  55
9.    D. G. Dix The Shape Of The Liturgy  A & C Black
      1986  48
10.   Ibid  238

11.     C. Cocksworth  Evangelical Eucharistic Thought ibid
        159-160
12.     M. Asthon ibid  96
13.     D. Stancliffe  ibid  X111
14.     M. Perham ibid  40, 43
15.     T. Hughes  ibid  15-16
16.     M. Perham  ibid  111-112
17.     Ibid  115
18.     K. Stevenson ibid  88-89
19.     A. Atherstone  Confesing Our Sins  Grove  2004  11
20.     C. Cocksworth & R. Brown  ibid  75
21.     T. Hughes  ibid  54-55
22.     D. J. Williams  Acts  Paternoster 1990  221
23.     M. Stringer  A Sociological Perspective Of Christian
        Worship  CUP  2005  238-239

# BIBLIOGRAPHY

A. Atherstone  Confessing Our Sins  Grove  2004

P. Atkins  Memory & Liturgy  Ashgate  2004

C. K. Barrett  John's Gospel  Westminster  Press 1978

J. Blenkinsopp  Ezekiel  J. Knox Press 1990

D. L. Block  Ezekiel  Ch. 1-24  Eerdmans  1997

J. M. Boice  John  Vol 1  Ch. 1-4  Baker  2000

M. E. Boring  Revelation  J. Knox Press 1989

I Boxall  Revelation  Continuum  2006

P. O'Brien  Philippians  Eerdmans  1991

C. G. Broyles  Psalms  Paternoster  2002

R. E. Brown  John  Ch. 1-12  Anchor  1966

F. F. Bruce  Hebrews  Eerdmans  1990

W. Brueggemann  Israel's Praise  Fortress Press 1988

W. Brueggemann  The Message Of The Psalms  Augsburg  1984

W. Brueggeman  The Psalms –The Life Of Faith  Fortress  Press  1995

W. Brueggemann  Isaiah  Ch. 1-39  J. Knox Press  1998

W. Brueggeman  Jeremiah  Eerdmans  1998

D. A. Carson  John  IVP  1991

D. A. Carson  Editor  Worship  Zondervann  2002

S. Christou  The Priest & The People Of God
Phoenix Books  2003

C. Cocksworth & R. Brown Being A Priest Today
Canterbury Press  2002

C. Cocksworth  Evangelical Eucharistic Thought In
The Church Of England  CUP  2002

C. Cocksworth  Holy, Holy, Holy – Worshipping The
Trinitarian God  DLT  2004

C. Cocksworth  Holding Together Catholic Evangelical
Worship In The Spirit  Lecture in Anvil  Vol 22 NO 1 2005

E. P. Clowney  1 Peter  IVP  1988

Common Praise Hymns  Canterbury Press 2000

P. H. Davids  1 Peter  Eerdmans  1990

M. J. Dawn Reaching Out Without Dumbing Down
Eerdmans  1995

T. Dearborn & S. Coll Editors  Worship At The Next
Level  Baker  2004

N. Due  Created For Worship  Mentor  2005

J. D. G. Dunn The Theology Of Paul The Apostle
Eerdmans  1998

W. Eichdrot  Ezekiel  Westminster Press  1970

P. Ellingworth  Hebrews  Eerdmans  1993

G. Fee  Philippians  Eerdmans  1995

F. Ford & D. W. Hardy  Living In Praise  DLT  2005

J. Gledhill  Leading A Local Church In The Age Of The
Spirit  SPCK  2003

D. Gregory Dix  The Shape Of The Liturgy  A & C Black
1986

V. P. Hamilton  Genesis  Ch. 18-50  Eerdmans  1995

Hawthorne: Martin: Reid: Dictionary of Paul & His Letters
IVP  1993

A. Hill  Enter His Courts With Praise – Biblical Principles
For Worship Renewal  Kingsway  1998

P. Hocken  Streams Of Renewal – The Origins &
Development Of The Charismatic Movement In
Great Britain  Paternoster  1997

M. Hooker  Paul  Oneworld  Oxford  2004

T. Hughes  Passion For Your Name  Kingsway  2004

E. James  A Life Of Bishop John A. T. Robinson  Collins
1987

G. Kendrick  Worship  Kingsway  1984

G. Kendrick  The G. Kendrick Collection 150 Songs
World Wide  2000

D. Kennedy  Understanding Anglican Worship  Grove  1997

C. R. Koester  Hebrews  Anchor  2001

C. Kroeker  Music In Christian Worship  Liturgical Press
2005

G. E. Ladd  Revelation  Eerdmans  1972

J. Leach  Liturgy & Liberty  Monarch  1989

J. Lucarni  Why I Left The Contemporary Christian
Music Movement  Evangelical Press  2002

J. R. Lundbom  Jeremiah Ch. 1-20  Anchor  1999

J. L. Mays  Amos  SCM  1969

J. L. Mays  The Psalms  J. Knox Press  1994

P. Moger  Music & Worship Principles To Practice
Grove  1994

L. Morris  John  Eerdmans  1995

J. A. Motyer  Amos  BST  1974

J. N. Oswalt  Isaiah Ch. 1-39  Eerdmans  1986

N. Page  And Now Let's Move Into A Time Of
Nonsense  Continuum  2004

A. Park  To Know You More  Kingsway  2003

R. Parry  Worshipping Trinity  Continuum  2005

M. Perham  New Handbook Of Pastoral Liturgy – A
Guide To Common Worship  SPCK  2000

D. Peterson  Engaging With God – A Biblical Theology
Of Worship  IVP  1992

M. Pilavachi  For The Audience Of One  Hodder  1999

C. Plantinga Jr. & S. A. Rozeboom  Discerning The
Spirits  Eerdmans  2003

M. Ramsey  The Christian Priest  SPCK  1985

M. Redman  Facedown  Kingsway  2005

M. Redman  The Unquencable Worshipper  Kingsway  2001

R. Redman  The Great Worship Awakening  Jossey-Bass  2002

Q. J. Schultz  High-Tech Worship  Baker  2004

D. J. Simundson  Amos  Abingdon  2005

Smail, Walker, Wright  Charismatic Renewal  SPCK  1993

Soul Survivor Songbook –  Survivor  2001

Soul Survivor Songbook –  Survivor  2006

Spring Harvest Songbook – 2006-2007

D. Stancliffe  God's Pattern – Shaping Our Worship,
Ministry & Life  SPCK  2003

J. Steven  Worship In The Restoration Movement
Grove  1989

J. H. S. Steven  Worship In The Spirit – Charismatic
Worship In The Church Of England  2002

K. Stevenson  Do This – The Shape, Style & Meaning Of The Eucharist  Canterbury Press  2002

M. Stringer  A Sociological History Of Christian Worship  CUP  2005

J. A. Thompson  Jeremiah  Eerdmans  1980

J. R. Walton  Hymns  OUP  2003

P. Ward  Selling Worship – How What We Sing Has Changed The Church  Continuum  2005

P. Ward  Editor  The Rite Stuff  BRF  2004

A. Weiser  The Psalms  SCM  1962

C. Westermann  Praise & Lament In The Psalms J. Knox Press  1981

P. Westermeyer  Te Deum – The Church & Music Fortress Press  1998

J. F. White  Christian Worship  Abingdon  1986

D. J. Williams  Acts  Paternoster  2002

T. Winslow  The Song Of The Lord – Prophetic Singing Kingsway  1996

C. J. Wright  Ezekiel  IVP  2001

T. & R. Wright  Contemporary Worship  Abingdon  1997

D. Zscech  Extravagant Worship  Bethany  2003

# SUGGESTED READING

I have suggested these books that are in my resource library as they cover many interesting topics concerning worship.

J. Begbie  Theology, Music & Time  CUP  2000

J. Blackwell  The Sacred In Music  Lutterworth Press  1999

C. Bowater  The Believer's Guide To Worship
Kingsway  1993

E. R. Brink  Editor  Authentic Worship In A Changing
Culture  CRC  1997

C. Buchanan  Encountering Charismatic Worship
Grove  1977

C. Cocksworth & Jeremy Fletcher  The Spirit & Liturgy
Grove  1998

P. Craig-Wild  Making Worship Work  DLT  2002

M. J. Dawn  A Royal Waste Of Time  Eerdmans  1999

M. Earey  Worship Audit  Grove  1995

L. Giglio  The Air I Breathe  Kingsway  2003

R. Giles  Re-Pitching The Tent  Canterbury Press  1996

R. Giles  Creating Uncommon Worship  Canterbury
Press  2004

D. Hilborn  Editor Toronto In Perspective – Papers On The
New Charismatic Wave OF The 1990s  Paternoster  2001

D. R. Holeton  Editor  Renewing The Anglican Eucharist
Grove  1996

R. W. Hovda  Strong, Loving & Wise  Liturgical Press  1976

G. Hughes  Worship As Meaning  CUP  2003

G. W. Lathrop  Holy Things  Fortress Press  1998

J. Leach  Living Liturgy  Kingsway  1997

Lloyd, Moger, Sinclair, Vasey  Introducing The New
Lectionary  Grove  1997

M. Marshall  Free To Worship  Marshall & Pickering 1996

K. Pecklers SJ  Editor  Liturgy In A Postmodern World
Continuum  2003

M. & B. Redman  Blessed Be Your Name  Hodder  2005

P. Roberts  Alternative Worship In The Church Of England
Grove  1999

D. Saliers  Worship & Theology  Abingdon  1994

C. J. Schmidt  Too Deep For Words – A Theology Of
Liturgical Expression  J. Knox Press  2002

G. Wainwright & K. B. W. Tucker  The Oxford History Of
Christian Worship  OUP  2006

M. Welker  What Happens In Holy Communion
Eerdmans  2000

S. White  The Spirit Of Worship  DLT  1999